California Fashion Designers

C A

Art and Style

L I F O R N I A

F A S H I O N

D E S I G N E R S

Douglas Bullis

Gibbs M. Smith, Inc.
Peregrine Smith Books

Published 1987 by Gibbs M. Smith, Inc.,
P.O. Box 667, Layton, Utah 84041

Designed by Smith & Clarkson

Printed and bound in Japan

91 90 89 88 87   5 4 3 2 1

First Edition

Front cover photo: design by Kaisik
Wong, photo by Thierry Mugler, courtesy
L'Officiel de la Couture, 1981

Back cover photos: design by Michael
Casey, photo courtesy Alan Purcell; design
by Jean Cacicedo, photo by David Leach;
design by Susie Tompkins, photo by
Oliviero Toscani

**Library of Congress
Cataloging-in-Publication Data**

California fashion designers.

　　1. Costume designers—California. I.
Bullis, Douglas.
TT507.C33 1987　　　746.9'2'0922 [B]
87-2354

ISBN 0-87905-278-3 (pbk.)

To Katy
for whose beauty books as this shall always be written.

CONTENTS

ACKNOWLEDGMENTS   A book as complex as this cannot happen without help. Costume designer Lucinda Formyduval taught me more about the subtleties of fabrics and the delight of fine fabrication than I ever believed possible; more than anyone else she made this book possible. During the trying stages of information gathering, especially helpful were Diane Saeks, Gladys Perint-Palmer, Pat Durkin of James Galanos Furs in New York, James Galanos, Peggy Mendelson of Neiman-Marcus in San Francisco, Lois Jensen and Randall Harris of San Francisco Fashion Industries, Sue Grunenwald and Veronica Akins of the San Francisco Design Network, Beverly Miller of Navarro Alternatives, Michael Casey, Karen Alexander, Sandra Sakata of Obiko, Frank and Anne Vigneri, Amanda Fuegi of Janet Orsi Public Relations, Liz Mecham and Brielle of Esprit, Karen Fortier of Bianculli, Jane Yamashita and Liz Rivers of Laurel Burch, Carol LaValley of Dennis Goldsmith, Jeanne Taylor and Jo Schuman of Lilli Ann, Rebecca Arum of Gunne Sax, and Paul Schnell of Ernst Strauss. Three remarkable women from the Modern Art Council of the San Francisco Museum of Modern Art—Rosemary Klebahn, Ann Roth, and Elise Phillips—were invaluable liaison with the many people in the Bay Area who appreciate California fashion as an art form. Special thanks should go to John Davis and Buckley Jeppson of Peregrine Smith Books, who provided invaluable editorial support.

INT

his is the first book to have been devoted to the fashion designers of California. Why should it have taken so long to arrive?

One obstacle was the magnitude of the task. California has inspired a tremendous number of people to design, paint, sculpt, write, and otherwise try to capture its spirit of place. The art of fashion design is no exception. California's 325-company, 15,000-employee garment industry forms its own $4 billion-a-year economy, can be said to have defined the term "casual wear" to millions of Americans, and boasts such names as James Galanos, Esprit, Gunne Sax, Guess?, Laurel Burch, Karen Alexander, Jeanne-Marc, and Lilli Ann. A major consideration, quite simply, was where to begin.

Another obstacle was that California fashion has too often been painted with the "regional" brush. Fashion critics rarely fly in from New York or Europe to review California seasons. Even locally, with the exception of a few perceptive writers such as Diane Saeks and Gladys Perint-Palmer, the California press gushes more ink on gossip from Italy than on innovators on their doorstep. For better or for worse, California fashion has been left to define itself.

Yet California fashion designers can hardly be called regionalists. In plain point of fact, no designer *dares* be regional in a business with such huge capital requirements, horrendous marketing costs, and knowledgeable consumers. The cash flow of the garment business guarantees one thing: aesthetic visions are either on the mark or there is an immediate batch of new ideas to replace them. Anyone might turn out to be a James Galanos or Jessica McClintock, and anyone can vanish without a trace after a first season. In today's international community, fashion centers aren't located on maps, they are located in people.

This book was subtitled "Art and Style" to emphasize the two major elements of California's complex fashion world. Here, too, are some misconceptions. It is tempting to think of San Francisco as the art-to-wear capital of the world, filled with specialists creating hand-painted fabrics and one-of-a-kind garments, and Los Angeles as the style capital of the West, filled with multinational corporations creating five lines a season. These descriptions don't fit reality. Four of the state's largest manufacturers are in San Francisco, and four of its most innovative art-to-wear designers are in Los Angeles. California fashion defies category, and for that is the better.

Much of this is due to the unpredictability of youth. California fashion has become an entity unto itself only recently. It has no centuries-old couture tradition to define aesthetics for generations of matrons, no bustling garment district, no sales reps leaking secrets to an ambitious army of journalists. No trade group sits down with a

PMS color fan and decides what color everybody's going to get next year.

Rather, California's surroundings, its special spirit of place, its busy populous sunlands and vast empty spaces, are what inspire these designers.

Yet when California designers do look abroad, they look more often to the East than the West. Art critics have long noted that California's cultural potpourri is making it America's first Pacific Rim art community. California designers are as comfortable in the Los Angeles/San Francisco/Tokyo/Hong Kong design axis as East Coast designers are with Milan/Paris/London/New York. Singapore factories manufacture goods for Esprit, Neiman-Marcus, Saks Fifth Avenue, and Macy's. The complex layered colors of Annie Hall's baggy pants and oversize shirts were monasticized into complex layered blacks by Rei Kawakubo of Comme des Garcons, whose fans among California designers promptly retinted her ideas but simplified their forms, which they then reexported to Singapore, where they were turned into batik motifs by William Lam. It is no surprise that many influential California fashion shows have been mounted not in Dusseldorf hotels or Milan trade centers but in Osaka art galleries.

The principle behind this book is that designers speak best for themselves. Each was asked these questions: Why are you doing what you do? Why do you think of it as art? What is fashion really all about? How did you get to be where you are?

The designers are each represented by a portrait, photographs of their work, a personally written biography, and a personal assessment of what they feel about their art, their business, their visions, anxieties, joys.

There are a number of people here who are almost unknown outside their own communities. This is particularly true of California's art-to-wear designers. These come closer to the European couture tradition of personalized wardrobes, perfect construction, handmade garments, and a respect for culture than anyone else California offers, with the exception of James Galanos. The fact that there is a healthy market for people whose work exists for aesthetic rather than business reasons points up several important things about the California fashion marketplace.

First is the existence of a market sizeable and reliable enough to keep so many limited-production designers alive. Artisans who produce one piece a month must price it accordingly. Fortunately for them, California has a huge number of people who think of fashion in wholly other terms than seasonal collections. To them, dressing to express an aesthetic is more important than dressing to stay warm. The personality in their wardrobe doesn't depend on the poses in fashion ads or being "in" or "out" this season.

Second, the principle rule that guides California fashion is that there are no rules. Designers suffer fewer restraints than in other fashion centers. The incestuousness of a longstanding network of designers, manufacturers, and journalists hardly exists. The number of successful designers with little or no formal schooling in "the industry" who started by selling on street corners or walking into Macy's with their entire production of twenty garments should encourage everyone except fashion merchandising teachers. Whatever aesthetic judgments may be placed on the work of California's limited-production designers, their sales say one thing clearly: In California there is a market for visionaries.

Third, nobody can survive in a vacuum. The success of many people in this book is linked to the willingness of equally visionary retailers and buyers to take chances. Sandra Sakata of Obiko in San Francisco has introduced more new designers than perhaps any other retailer. Laurel Burch, Michael Casey, Jeanne Allen, Joseph Abbati, and many others got their start by phoning up Macy's or Saks Fifth Avenue and asking for an appointment with the buyer. J. Magnin's buyers supported many people in this book in the early 1970s when many younger designers were first prying their images loose from hippiedom.

Finally, the observation that Californians create their history instead of inheriting it has been worn smooth with use, but is true nonetheless. For a long time New York's fashion sensibility was defined largely by artists and designers who fled Europe before World War II. That sensibility looked to the past for its identity. California is free from that. These designers' very lack of history inspires a search for the timeless, driven by the urge to create new ideas.

JOS

E P H A B B A T I

**SAXON
MEN'S WEAR,
SAN FRANCISCO**

This one-piece bike
suit for winter riding is
made of wool jersey.

am attracted to cool or deep colors, perhaps because of San Francisco's climate. San Francisco is a city with a very complex personality. The absence of dominant seasons focuses one on subtleties. Moody summers and foggy evenings direct me to colors such as indigo, colors with blue bases, colors that act as complements to people's warm complexions. I also like natural shades of white, but for my own personal dress I prefer black so my clothes become secondary to my being.

I respond to fabrics that hold their shape with a minimum of support. In outerwear I like working with heavy coatings such as wool melton and blanket-weight textiles, especially in the fall. I admire the way the fluidity of gabardines accents body movements. Similarly, I use knits such as double-weight jersey for its movement and comfort.

My recent spring and summer collections have made extensive use of traditional Japanese fabrics such as *shijira* and *tsumugi* (striped cottons) because of their exceptional quality and uniqueness in the American market. Many fine Japanese fabrics produced in limited quantities by cottage industries weren't exported until I started using them.

I like to juxtapose. For example, I'll combine heavy woolens with bridal satins in fall outerwear. Satin helps coats slide on and off easily and conveys a subtle hint of hidden luxury. I find the sponge-like quality of knitwear very comfortable because of its cushiony texture. I also like the uneven texture of handwoven textiles because of the human imprint their slight inconsistencies place on the fabric.

My designs are evolutionary and build as one's wardrobe does. Over the last five years I've accumulated a group of designs for outerwear, shirts, pants, vests, and sweaters that I consider the core of a wardrobe which evolves gradually season through season. By considering design as continuous I can graft an idea inspired by a new fabric onto something familiar.

Many times during the course of researching fabrics I'll come across a material or a weave that can transform one of my basic designs into something entirely new, yet retain its essence. When I came across Japanese *shijira* I was told that it was traditionally used for summer kimonos. Its seersucker texture and its lightness made it perfect for a summer suit. The result was a suit that feels like pajamas, yet holds its shape as well as a heavier semi-constructed design. Conversely, if I feel that shape is my key goal, I'll find textiles that can accomplish my intended effect.

I love fashion design because it is such an evolutionary process. It has enabled me to mark the times of my life and our culture. I chose to design menswear because I believe it is the most exciting

This semi-constructed suit uses a Japanese *shijira* fabric that I designed.

Wool melton collarless sport jacket.

and challenging area of fashion design. The possibilities for change and for pioneering new ideas are endless. I also like the pace at which men's fashion evolves. Changes come about on a more human level and they generally remain current much longer.

I moved from Michigan to California in 1976 and spent two years in Sacramento before coming to San Francisco. I recall the

This unconstructed cardigan jacket was designed to go with full pleated pants and a wool gabardine shirt.

Wool gabardine is a recurring fabric in my collections, as with this three-button sport jacket and tailored pant.

exact moment when I knew clothing design would be my career. I had just graduated from training in hair styling and was preparing to move to San Francisco. I happened to be sewing some pants for myself and was suddenly struck by the revelation that this is what I would be doing for the rest of my life. I hadn't the faintest idea how to begin a fashion career but I knew that's what I'd be doing.

When I got to San Francisco I found a position at the Vidal Sassoon salon. At that time I was designing clothes for myself, more for my personal pleasure than anything else. A group of us who experimented in creative ways of personal adornment staged a fashion show. Shortly thereafter a local tabloid interviewed me as a designer. All this excitement and attention started me thinking of taking design more seriously, so I pursued it.

I decided to concentrate on menswear. I presented my first collection in 1981 at a local art gallery and found a store to carry my collection. The next year I took my collection to New York and got an editorial photo in *G Q* magazine. I didn't sell anything that first trip, but persevered and made sales on subsequent showings. Eventually I became involved with trade shows in New York, Paris, and Los Angeles.

I am inspired by designers who are artists, whose aesthetics are articulations of well-conceived philosophic beliefs. There are many fashion stylists who are good at embellishing an existing fashion trend, but far fewer designers have original insights. Giorgio Armani comes to mind as one of the latter. He has originated a style that was previously unknown. I regard him as the most mature and contemporary European designer. Rei Kawakubo of Comme des Garcons creates a sophistication I am very impressed with. At times her designs can look traditional, yet her innovative use of proportion, textiles, and details makes her garments truly original. I also like Agnes B.'s premise that clothing should be comfortable and functional first.

Other art forms also motivate my work. Fashion is but one part of a culture's totality. People speak to each other in myriad ways using physical expressions—poetry, writing, song, advertising, film, video, and so on. That's why I look at clothing as art. I believe art and design can be thought of as two separate entities, but the postmodernist movement has changed many people's interpretation of art, and many designers are considered as artists.

I work in San Francisco because its climate, quality of life, and ambience are most suited to my own way of life. California still has a pioneer spirit that enables people to develop new ideas. That is very important to me. When I travel it's usually not for specific inspirations but rather an affirmation of the influence California has upon me. I'm always happy to get back here.

*T*ropicana Dress.

K A R

*T*ea Party Dress.

*B*ronco Dress.

EN ALEXANDER

**SHADY GROVE,
OAKLAND**

ashion is directly influenced by current events and the way we evolve as they happen. I selected these images to show the growth in my designs as I grew within. I also wanted to express how much I have been changed by the changes in our times.

Many designers of the 1960s were influenced by the peace movement. I was one of them. I matured a great deal in that era, and was struck by the flower child nostalgia for a prettier, more meaningful, less stressed life. I designed many lace-up peasant dresses with a free, unstructured, barefoot feeling.

Despite my design changes over the years I produced an unbroken succession of housedresses. Several of them appear here. Their genesis goes back to the 1940s, when I was influenced by the way my mother dressed. She designed all her own clothes. I remember reproaching her to wear dresses instead of skirts or pants. Then *I* ended up as a dress designer.

In college I was a painting major at the University of Denver. I often found myself looking through the latest *Vogue* magazine instead of *Art News*. When I finished school I kept painting and sewing for myself. Then I began to do hand-painted dresses. A friend opened a store and I sewed for her—fourteen hours a day. My clothes began selling and that was the beginning of my career.

My vision is of shape. The role of line is so important it can be compared only with sculpture, for after all, a fashion design is sculpture that can walk. My eyes are the rulers, T-squares, putty, and calculus that end in the silhouette that will make the person I am dressing look perfect.

The look I love in a woman is of broad shoulders, small waist, voluptuous hips, and long legs. This has been my aesthetic for seventeen years, to the point of having become my trademark. Yet it isn't easy to accomplish my (or any) intended vision. A quarter of an inch difference in shoulder line can ruin an effect.

Fashion is like a wheel which rotates through a season. Color is a reflection of the wheel's passing. If I design in black one season, chances are I will design in white the next. If one year's work is in bright primaries, the next's will likely be in pastels and medium brights. I balance a color wheel of blue and green and red and gray, with minor characters of yellow, pink, aqua, and mauve.

For me fabric must be natural. My clothes must be comfortable and breathe easily, with a loose, free sense of fun. Cottons have a relaxed freedom. I love working in rayon because it is very drapy—a good medium for housedresses. I can use it to combine great floppy sleeves and collars with tight, sexy waists and hips, then free flares to the bottom for movement and flow.

Diamond Wrap Dress.

    Accessories are not important to me. My design must stand alone, to work by itself. I design dresses that employ fabric as architects employ steel: without knowing the properties of tensile strength and ductility, a building won't stand. I try to create an image complete enough that it lacks only shoes. Whatever else the wearer adds is for that person's fun and personal expression.

    Designs come to me spontaneously. I have sketched on a napkin in a restaurant, in a taxi, on a theatre program. Once I was vexed with the complexities of being more firm with my children, so I did an imaginary group of General Patton, MacArthur, and Eisenhower dresses. I have no formula for when and where my ideas will come. It is crucial to me that I be true to myself even at the risk

Flamingo Dress.

Cowgirl Dress.

Promenade Dress.

of failure because so many women experience situations similar to mine. I want my dresses to make each customer feel wonderful, to touch something special inside her and bring this specialness out.

I work on a day-by-day basis. I give my sketches to my patternmaker. She is like my best friend—sensitive to me and able to understand the feelings that are behind the sketch. She must also be very flexible and willing to redo everything on a dress until it works. For example, if I suddenly have a strong feeling for Victorian dresses in starchy flat white cotton, I will go to an old clothing store, buy an antique apron from the 1890s, and send it to a fabric vendor to reproduce the cloth to achieve the look I want. While the fabric is being made I try to find something close to its look and feel. I have that fabric dyed in colors that fit with the look I am trying to achieve. This is how I develop a collection. I do five such collections a year: transition, fall, cruise/holiday, spring, and summer. I design from 100 to 150 dresses a season. This translates to about ten weeks to realize a collection.

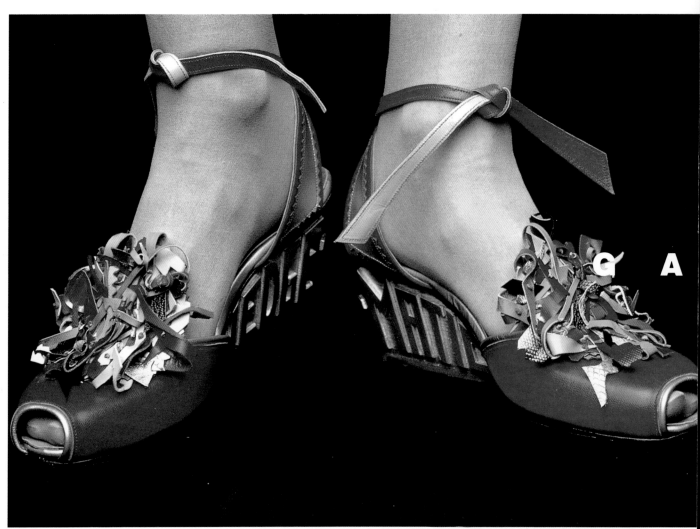

G   A

Wedge-A-Matics,
1983. Kidskin, exotic
leathers, wood,
linoleum, paint.

Baby Needs a New
Pair of Shoes, 1985.
Patent leather, kidskin,
soling leather, dice.

V find it unfortunate that some people have the mistaken idea that shoes are accessories. They are a necessity determined by function and are an integral part of one's total image.

I like the message, humor, or origin of my ideas to be recognizable, yet not intrude on the fact that the work is functionally and aesthetically successful.

Colors are very important to me. They elicit attitudes and emotions in me and my viewer. The discovery of the "right" color is often a struggle and almost always a surprise. Colors affect each other and work differently on different days.

At the moment I am attracted to leather—kidskin, snake, and lizard. These do everything I ask of them. I have yet to exhaust their potential.

Shoe designs sometimes pop into my head fully formed. More often only a little corner of an idea appears—perhaps a technique I'd like to explore further *(Lightning Strikes Twice)*, or a funny play on words *(Wedge-A-Matics)*, or a seductive material *(Never Say Never Again, Right, Den?)*. I sketch directly on the shoe last, which is covered with paper or canvas, often taping bits of leather here and there to see how the colors work. My choice of subject matter is often subconscious; material and color are emotional.

I have always made things. My parents instilled in me the idea that I could make anything I could think of. I still have that expectation—if I can dream it I can construct it.

I have no formal education in art or design. All my friends are artists and I have always been one. Sometimes other people's work inspires me, but more often it is their attitude or philosophy.

Z A   B O W E N

SANTA CRUZ

Inside-out Triangle Belt, 1985. Kidskin, brass Chicago screws, paint.

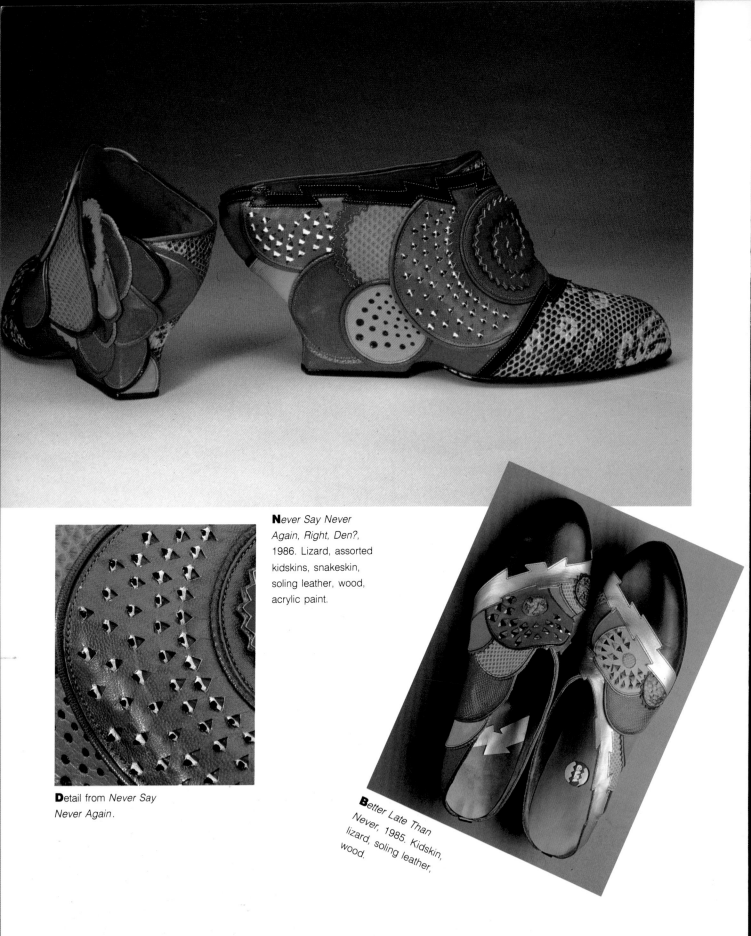

Never Say Never
Again, Right, Den?,
1986. Lizard, assorted
kidskins, snakeskin,
soling leather, wood,
acrylic paint.

Detail from Never Say
Never Again.

Better Late Than
Never, 1985. Kidskin,
lizard, soling leather,
wood.

Victorian Fan Compo-
nent Belt, 1985.
Component belts have
button-on pieces to
vary their length.

A Dose Of Her Own
Medicine Belt, 1982.

K.Lee, You're On
Your Own, 1983.
Kidskin, lizard, wine
corks.

Lightning Strikes
Twice, 1985. Snake
and kidskin, wood,
soling leather.

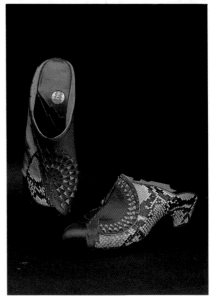

L A

Most of my designs
evolve. A thought
becomes a shape,
adds color, is carved
into a model, then
lives.

UREL BURCH

**LAUREL BURCH, INC.,
SAN FRANCISCO**

I realized I was a designer when I realized I could create something that enabled people to express their spirit.

once met a man in the jungles of Bali. We didn't have more than two or three words in common, but when he saw my drawings he threw his head back and his eyes sparkled, he beamed, his face was illuminated. His delight was universal. Now he carves the mythical menageries that cluster like shrines in my house, my shops, my displays. All ways of life increase one's sense of spirit. All offerings come back in such ways.

When I was a girl I used to collect little stones in bags. I delighted in their shapes and colors. When I got home I'd put them in different arrangements and love them. When I started school I'd rarely come straight home. I'd meander around, seeking secret hideouts I *knew* were full of treasures from other worlds. I remember always dreaming beyond what I knew, then coming up with something that made the dreams come true. When I was seven I put on circuses in my garage for the neighborhood kids. I'd collect money from them, and *then* figure out what I was going to do.

I ran away from home at fourteen and ended up in a Catholic boarding school. It was thirty nuns and me. I didn't have parents, I didn't have friends. I created my world out of imaginary cultures, other worlds, fantasy animals. I converted my convent room into the hideouts of my childhood. I'd put on a grass skirt and dance to recorded music from Bora Bora, read *The Prophet,* or pretend I was a flamenco dancer. Mother Superior didn't approve. I often wondered what she did with the grass skirt.

For the longest time nobody validated what I was doing. In high school I was the one with hair down to my waist, who made exotic coffees, who lit candles in my bedroom—and who wound up in the Haight in 1966 thanking the friends who sheltered me with gifts of necklaces and earrings of wire hammered into twists using the flat bottom of a frying pan I'd bought in the flea market. I shaped coins, beads, and bones I found on the street into things that looked as though they came from faraway peoples. I thought of them as the spirit of life that creation gives to all people.

I worked in a jewelry store for $1.25 an hour, of which fifty cents had to go for babysitting. I had no idea my own time had value, and I sold my own creations for $2.00 a pair. I thought having two kids stacked the deck against me, but by combining Egyptian beads, Chinese coins, and odds and ends from around the world I could hold onto my inside self.

It might have gone on that way forever, but one day I walked into a Ghirardelli Square store owned by Lois Smith, wearing a necklace of metal and beads I'd made. She loved it and got me to making and selling jewelry for her and other stores. I delivered my first pieces wrapped in Japanese mulberry paper and decorated my first invoices with drawings of little mythopoetic animals.

At first my reputation grew by word of mouth. Then I went to New York and bumped into an old friend, Cathy Hardwick. She took one look at the jewelry on my neck (overlooking the baby strapped to my back) and said, "Come on, we're going to *Vogue*." The result was two pages of photos in *Vogue* and three pages in *Harper's Bazaar*. Ironically, no one could buy those pieces because they were all I had.

Then I had a chance to travel to some of the exotic Far Eastern places I had always dreamed of. In 1971 a friend showed my work to some officials in mainland China. They invited me there and introduced me to their cloisonné. I was awed by how a technique of such immense heritage, spanning the world from Egypt to China over two thousand years, could result in an exquisite beauty that seemed timeless. First they made a die, then imprinted it on copper. Each color was applied with a tiny spatula, then fired. Color by color, firing by firing, each piece grew. Then they were filed smooth by hand and fired again for a gloss, hand rubbed again, plated with gold or silver, and finally polished again. I immediately saw my designs blossoming in cloisonné, and we settled on terms. I still like to think that the fact I was doing business with China a year before Nixon proves that art precedes politics!

Back at home, by 1974 my little five-helper business had to move from the kitchen table into the garage. I couldn't design fast enough. I'd break to cook lunch, using spices I'd collected overseas. Then I discovered through a soured business partnership that the relationship I really wanted was between business and art. This rela-

Jewelry gives you the challenge of conveying an enormous amount of meaning in a tiny space.

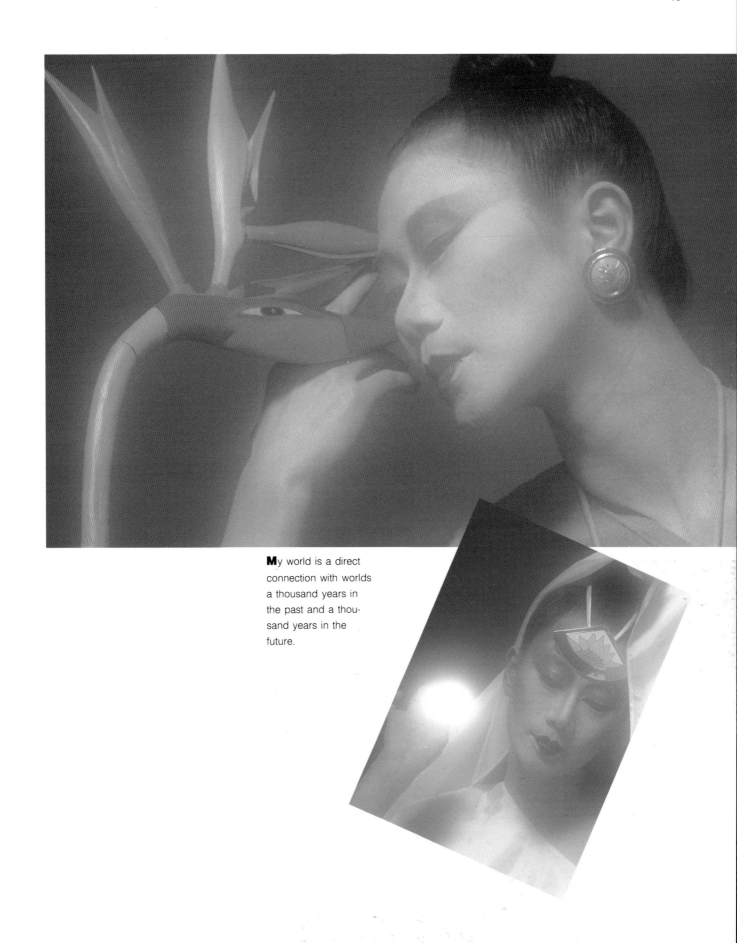

My world is a direct
connection with worlds
a thousand years in
the past and a thou-
sand years in the
future.

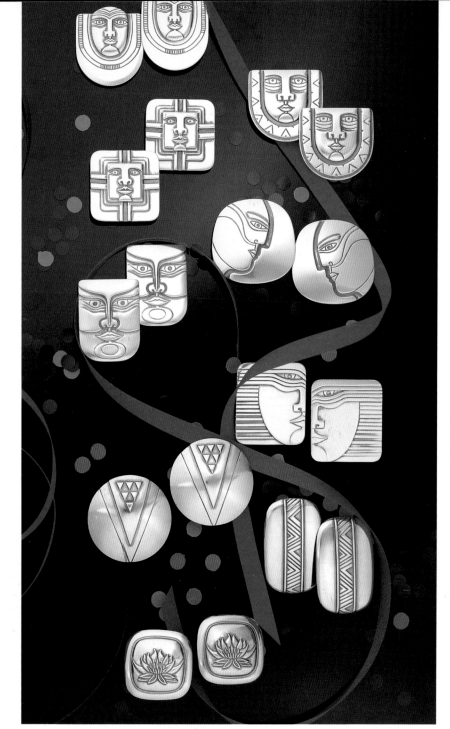

If my design fulfills the person wearing it, it fulfills me.

tionship became so harmonious that I discovered my business instinct was something I loved.

Part of my philosophy is designing the environment in which my work appears—stores within stores that have a unique identity that raises my work from display into environment. Stores have been very responsive to this idea. I feel it vital to expand design from concept to environment. Designers usually create only a product, not the circumstances in which it is presented. I integrate design with the place where it is displayed, bought, wrapped, presented. Presentation is as much a part of the design as the design itself. This is a direct extension of my spirit, of my personal relationship with the wearer.

Though I don't think of myself as a fashion designer, I *am* an artist, and artists are communicators. Their spirit is form. My spirit is bringing people together. If I create something so special people give it as they do themselves, then they also give me. That's the most meaningful thing I can do.

Sometimes my designs come to mind fully formed. Most of the time they evolve. A thought becomes a shape, adds color, becomes an idea, a sketch, a carving, a model, a being. In jewelry, you don't have yards of fabric. You have perhaps one inch which has to capture and convey an enormous amount of meaning. I started with amulets. I loved their spirit. I felt beautiful when someone else felt beautiful. Magic was their core. My job was to unveil it. The wearer received it in his or her own way.

Cloisonné gave me the ability to create a minature which captures an enormity. That hasn't changed. My world is a direct connection with worlds that existed thousands of years ago and will exist thousands of years hence. I always knew there was a universal plan that somehow could be captured in my work. What surprised me was that it was wanted by so many others.

Cut Out Series vest with scarf. Felted wool, appliqué, knit.

Night in the Garden. Felted wool, appliqué, knit.

e are heirs to a tradition of colorful costume whose heritage has been so undermined as to have been nearly lost. In our era of mass-manufactured, mass-advertised clothing and five fashion seasons a year, we are supposed to not only look like the model in the ad, we are supposed to think we *should* look like that.

My aesthetic is very different. Like Leon Bakst, the costume and set designer for the Ballets Russes in the 1910s, my intent is to create a living fantasy, a work of art in each garment, a unique character whose presence draws out the wearer's spirit. This philosophy is based on combining in one design a functional piece of clothing with aesthetic fantasy. The designs shown here illustrate my attitude that art and the act of wearing can be one in the same; that wearability, comfort, warmth, and style are as important as beauty.

N   C A C I C E D O

BERKELEY

I am not interested in mass production. It is important to me to maintain the utmost of quality control in each garment while satisfying the many people who want something unique.

Color is exceptionally important to me. I want color to exist not merely on the surface but all through the material, saturating it. The reason I personally dye most of my fabrics is to control the subtleties of its gradation and to increase my palette.

My imagery is largely derived from colorful landscapes and textural forms in nature. I mostly work with outerwear. My designs begin with several sketches. Most derive from the traditional flat pattern shapes of the Japanese kimono. The simplicity of the T shape allows me to concentrate on the surface design of the overall "canvas." The basic concept is first transferred onto a muslin pattern to check the fit and styling of each shape, then onto a life-size paper pattern on which I draw the design directly. Then I consider the choice of fabrics and colors—dyeing and felting (shrinking) are the most significant parts of a piece's design and construction.

Portrait, 1986 in jacket made in collaboration with K.Lee Manuel. Painted leather with wool.

I prefer very textural fabrics. Wool is my favorite. It is warm, durable, and is available in an extraordinary range of weights and textures. It is also extremely resilient and has a superb affinity for dyes. Felting produces a soft, dense fiber which is most suitable to the designs I construct. Appliquéing felted wool produces a clean sharp edge that works perfectly with the shapes I use.

I then drench the fabric in hot- and cold-water baths to bring about the greatest shrinkage. Hot-water dyes help this process and give me an unlimited palette. My preference is the warm palette of earth tones. The fabric is then cut, pieced, and stitched to my pattern. I'll often emphasize the design with appliqué, sometimes sewn from the reverse side then shorn away from the top surface to produce a crisp edge. Striped knitted bands "frame" many of my designs—they're a signature of my work. One reason for this is that the edges of my garments are often curvilinear and nonsymmetrical; finishing bands maintain the sharpness of these edges.

I graduated from the Pratt Institute in New York with a Bachelor of Fine Arts in Sculpture in 1970. My work derives from this strong academic background in painting and sculpture. I was one of the first students at Pratt to use textiles as a sculptural medium. I began to create one-of-a-kind clothing based on my fascination with the human form and with the symbols of traditional costume. These became the foundation on which my imagery could move and interact with space.

The first technique I used was crochet, which enabled me to paint and sculpt with any yarn I desired. The very process of crochet is much like drawing—stitches make lines, lines make shapes, shapes

Chaps—A Cowboy Dedication. Felted wool, appliqué, knit.

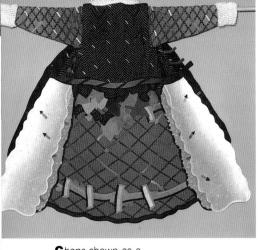

Chaps shown as a wall decoration on a dowel.

Black Leaves. Felted wool, appliqué, knit.

Art Deco Coat. Felted wool, appliqué, knit.

make forms. However, over the years crochet began to be too bulky, too wooly, too organic for the graphic imagery I was inventing. I began collecting white fabrics that could be dyed, cut, and stitched to achieve greater visual dimensions than a flat surface.

I came to California to find a new and different life. California at that time (1970) was a mecca for textile artists. It was an exhilarating place to be, a marvelously supportive environment where I felt free to experiment with the multitude of different techniques my medium made possible.

Sunset Coat. Felted
wool, appliqué, knit.

Joanne's Coat. Felted
wool, appliqué, knit.

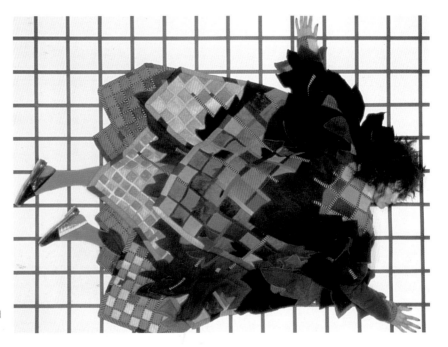

Checkerboards. Felted
wool, appliqué, knit.

New Jersey Dress.
Wool jersey with
reverse wool appliqué.

In 1972 I moved to Wyoming to experience yet another new world. I learned to focus my ideas, to find my inner strength and beliefs. It was the most prolific period of my life. I minimized external influences and concentrated on invention, development, experiment.

Eight years later I returned to California, where there is endless support for adventuring within one's art form. I am also drawn here to be among people whose passion for beauty and expression matches mine. I love the many artists and designers I know here, not just for their work but for who they are, the style in which they live, the essence of life they embody. But more than that, there is a subliminal desire to capture the timeless. I am not concerned with "fashionable" garments but rather with clothing that unites being worn, being put on a wall as art, being appreciated year after year, and being at one with the costume tradition that commenced when someone realized clothing was more than just warmth.

Transformations.
Crochet, knit, leather.

E L E

One of my favorite
styles is the dress that
fits like a second skin.

ore champagne, old boy?" The tall, dark, and handsome millionaire playboy Guy Wainwright stood before me in a chic white dinner jacket, offering a chilled glass of Dom Perignon.

"No thanks, Wainwright, I'll stick to rye," I replied as I surveyed the bustling casino floor below me. "Go on with your story."

"Ah, yes. Well, the last time I saw the Countess Casadei was at a gala fashion show I held at my villa to unveil her latest collection. Such a collection! Smouldering metallics that heated up the night! A slinky matte jersey cocktail dress shirred from shoulders to hem! A fabulous crinkly-lamé bustier with a mermaid silhouette, flounce skirt, and pleated bodice reminiscent of the stars of the silver screen! Sparkling jewels! Seductively bare halter dresses!"

T R A   C A S A D E I

LOS ANGELES

Then Wainwright's voice dropped. "Unfortunately, amid the confusion and excitement, the famed Von Heisling jewels were stolen and the Countess vanished in the night. I've been frantically searching for her ever since."

"Do you think she stole the jewels?"

"No, not the jewels," Wainwright confessed, "but definitely my heart. I've got to see her again."

Not one to see a grown man cry, I quickly changed the subject. "There's no one I can't find, as long as the price is right."

Wainwright, paying no attention to my immodest boasting, continued with his lament. "She's a devastating creature. Tall and willowy with jet black hair and piercing eyes. Her signature is the line of seductively feminine dresses she designs. Silhouettes that are lean, bare, and inviting. Fabrics that drape, shirr, and cling to the body like a second skin. Elaborate beading and detailing beyond compare. Trust me, you'll know her when you see her. The Casadei woman has a style all her own."

I was getting a little confused listening to Wainwright's description. What exactly was I looking for? A woman—or a style of dressing? Only time would tell.

Clustered around the baccarat table below were some very lovely—and very likely—suspects. A sultry brunette in a black halter dress was captivating the entire Austrian polo team. Another enchantress in a printed gold lamé entranced a Count, a Viscount, and a no-count (a swindler, I suspected). Suspect Number Three was a voluptuous vixen in a slinky matte jersey cocktail dress. As she nuzzled on the ear of a Brazilian race car driver, every pair of eyes in the room, including mine, were on her.

Here was the problem: All these women fit Wainwright's description to a T! Seductive, alluring, sensuous females in dresses guaranteed to stop traffic, if not an aging millionaire's heart. Any one of them could be the Casadei woman. The question was, which one?

I continued to survey the room until I finally zeroed in on the prime candidate. This one had to be Countess Casadei—I just knew it. I quickly reviewed her background—having received her B.A. in

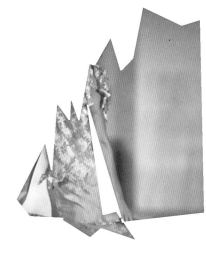

My signature is the seductive dress for the glamorous, alluring, irresistible woman.

marketing from California State University, she was working as a buyer for a Santa Barbara specialty shop chain and getting her master's in business from Loyola, when her fiancé, Rick Lieberman, suggested she design her own line. My mouth went dry, my heart began to pound against the silver-handled .45 nestled safely in my shoulder holster. Like a hunter stalking his prey, I edged down the stairs. Then I stood face to face with this tantalizing temptress. She wore an off-the-shoulder gunmetal lamé dinner dress. "Countess Casadei, I presume," I said with wry satisfaction.

"Countess—Ha! I only wish!" she replied as she threw back her head and laughed.

"But your dress!" I stammered.

"Eletra Casadei, my dear," she purred. "Devastating dresses for the Countess in all of us."

M I C

My early interest in
theatrical costume
design helps to explain
the drama and wear-
ability of my gowns.

H A E L C A S E Y

**MICHAEL CASEY
COUTURE,
SAN FRANCISCO**

was interested in drama and theatrical costume long before I came to fashion design. The demands of theatre discipline a designer in ways traditional fashion training cannot. Performance is a world where clothing must be true to its function but also comfortable. Performers do stretches, falls, embraces, chases, dances, and a dozen other things people don't do in daily life. You quickly learn the limits of materials and fabrication, and how to adapt to director demands or last-minute changes to a plot.

Theatre also taught me the inherent limitations of effects. Skillful lighting can't tell a tale. A sure sign of the uncertain technician is someone striving for effect. Effect for itself dazzles but detracts from acting. It doesn't move the audience to believe.

I've translated these lessons into fashion in many ways. Body consciousness, comfort, and durability are the first things I consider. The garment must adapt to the wearer's many activities. Only after these basics are taken care of do I start thinking of lines and shapes that will remain stylish for years. I take industry trends into consideration, but gimmicks inherently eliminate themselves.

I try to combine the skillful with the subtle such that the wearer is center stage without grabbing the limelight. Too much of anything robs the very memorableness he or she is trying to achieve. Part of my philosophy comes from costume history. The styles of the 1920s through 1940s were ingeniously cut, but they were memorable because they were wearable.

Many of my designs are inspired by fabrics. I look for character, for complex or unique qualities, for fabrics that can lift an ordinary silhouette or shape into the extraordinary—silk jacquard, lamé, Italian double-weight, satin-faced organza, silk-cut velvet, four-ply silk crepe, French reembroidered lace, or taffetas. These take on incredible life when enhanced with iridescent colors.

I like to embellish my gowns with generous amounts of hand beading. I love to orchestrate incongruous textures; for example, combining lavishly sensual beaded velvet with stiff taffeta. I'll also take a fabric one step further—adding beading to embroidered lace or smocking a lamé. This often means sacrificing the quantity of production to the quality of an extraordinary fabric, but classic designs become memorable in part because they take such risks.

The most enduring lesson I got from theatre is the direct relationship between myself and the person who wears my work. I want to enhance the woman, not overpower her. Although I've been known in the past for body-conscious fitting, now I'm experimenting with looser styles and separates. But drama and wearability will remain absolutes I won't discard. I don't make dresses to defy the

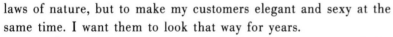

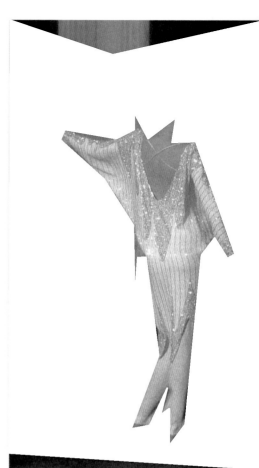

laws of nature, but to make my customers elegant and sexy at the same time. I want them to look that way for years.

Hence I place a great deal of value in comments made by customers and store buyers. I want to know why styles sell well—not because I want to imitate them but to find the resonance they strike in their wearers. I am especially interested in variations on a theme. If a dress has sold reasonably well, but a modified version with a shorter skirt or sleeveless arm suddenly sells spectacularly well, I look for the reasons why.

I was raised in Austin, Texas. From a very early age I wanted to be in theatre. I went to the University of Texas and the Traphagen School of Fashion in New York. After I graduated I got a job as a sketch artist and design assistant for television and ended up designing costumes for the Radio City Music Hall. That translated to over 250 costumes per show, everything from tap-dancing banana trees to Rockettes.

It was a wildly unpredictable world. My very first design was for Ginger Rogers—a lobster costume shaped like Mae West, complete with a parsley boa and a clam shell purse. The next day I had to design 75 identical beaded and fringed dance costumes.

Many of my designs are inspired by extraordinary, unique fabrics.

In 1981 I moved to the West Coast. Bill Ball of San Francisco's American Conservatory Theatre asked me to design costumes for his 1981-1982 season. That stretched into a tenure of fifteen plays, ranging from giggly period farces to gloomy Ibsen tragedies.

One of my hand-beaded gowns was auctioned to actress Marsha Mason at the 1984 ACT gala. Ingrid Weiss, a friend of mine, advised me to start designing fashions. Wilkes Bashford presented my first season's designs in his store. The next year he launched my second season at a San Francisco residence. That effectively set my sails as a designer.

These designs incorporate classic lines and shapes that I hope will remain elegant and stylish for years.

Vionnet. Made in collaboration with Ben Compton.

Embroidered Blouse and Skirt. Dip dyed hand embroidered silk.

Velvet Dress, shown at a San Jose Museum of Art exhibition in 1985.

he woman I design for is sensitive to fabric, to material handled in an unusual way. She has the self-confidence to wear something that goes beyond fashion. She expects a substantial amount of hand labor, detailing, and embellishment. I design what I feel she needs to nourish all of her being—her intellect, her femininity, her sensuality, her sense of daring.

My studio is in the Coast Range foothills near Los Gatos. I employ a patternmaker, sample makers, and special seamstresses, plus fabric printers and buttonmakers in California and England who create the unusual buttons I design to enhance my work. Mills in France and Italy weave custom yardage for me, other mills do my silk screens, and an assistant helps me with dyeing.

RIAN CLAYDEN

MARIAN CLAYDEN, INC., LOS GATOS

In 1964 I began experimenting with dyes and cloth. There was no specific moment when I decided I had become a fashion designer, although I was always interested in fashion and played with ideas in my own wardrobe. I did wall hangings and other fabric art for a long time. My work was included in an exhibit on the American interpretation of *shibori* (a Japanese form of resist dyeing) that traveled all over Japan. I have a piece in the permanent collection of the Victoria and Albert Museum in London, and have been in many international shows since 1970.

Garments and wall hangings are different aspects of the same idea. One sculpture moves, the other doesn't. One goes on to another life, the other carries its only life within itself. They have the same ability to move the beholder to appreciate what wasn't perceived before. But fashion can be rearranged and reinterpreted by the wearer and thus become a conversation between us. You can't do that with something on the wall.

I did my first collection in 1981, and for some time did only one collection a year. Now I do four—fall, holiday, resort, and spring/summer. I came from England influenced both by anti-fashion street clothes and by gorgeous traditional cloth. Over the years I developed a tremendous fascination with the designs and quality of Japanese textiles, with the vibrant colors and flowing lines of Middle Eastern cloth, and with the clean sophistication of the European silhouette. When I came to California everything loosened up. Each time I travel I come back with new ideas, but it seems natural that here in California have I been able to join the European, Oriental, and my own past influences into something cohesive and real. I find a spiritual freedom here that I didn't have in Europe. Now I can travel back to Europe and carry this precious possession that California gave me.

Almost from the beginning I was fascinated with the dyer's

art. I suppose that along with decorating pottery and adorning the body with clays, dyeing is one of the oldest crafts in the world. Dyeing is like dancing. My partner, the dye bath, has its own energy, its own expression, it creates something separate from my creativity. I can lead or follow. I must be willing to take chances. The results can surprise me and lead in new directions.

I want my garments to communicate not only about the surface but in other ways, too—color, fiber, texture, form, function, sensuality. First and foremost is the fabric. It often is the first thing to inspire me, it suggests the direction the garment should take. I'll use beautiful fabrics from France, Italy, and the Orient, then enhance them with dyeing techniques that include silk screen, clamp resist, and discharging, looking for an interplay that creates a special spark.

Thus I use dyeing to create an attitude in my work. It is the same with other designers I respect—Fortuny for his fabrics, Erté for line, Kansai Yamamoto for outrageousness. The images I create appear in different ways. A lily that appears one season may appear several seasons later as a discharge or resist effect, a silk screen, or a button. I'll recycle a silk screen design by using it with other colors and fabrics to create a new look which has its forebears in past seasons. If a fabric feels right for me I'll use it for years.

Here in California I am able to create work that combines the present and the past into a continuum, in the same way that dyeing is as contemporary as today yet is one of the oldest art forms. Some people feel a surge of enormous human continuity when they walk into a cathedral, others when they visit a long-lived culture such as one finds in Asia, Iran, or Morocco. For me, when a garment is complete and expresses everything I wanted yet has taken on something more, that is magic. That is an exquisite moment. Here is a strong, clear work made by me about this moment in time. I am at one with the earliest and most recent garments made by mankind.

Shiraz Dress. Hand silk-screened image of a Kashmir shawl, woven and printed in Como, Italy.

Mop Coat. Dip dyed cotton mop cloth.

Viennese Bias Dress. Hand woven in Lyon, France, dip dyed and shrunk.

Art-to-wear is an expression of emotion. There's a direct link between emotion and the garment.

M A

f men knitted, it would be called architecture. When I started I loved clothes but wanted to be recognized as an artist. There is as much challenge putting a jacket together as creating a Braun coffee maker.

I was born in Schenectady, New York, and got my degree in industrial design from the Pratt Institute in New York City in 1970. I was one of the original art-to-wear creators and have work in the collection of the Metropolitan Museum of Art.

I began concentrating on conceptual fine art pieces in 1978. Two years later a friend and *G Q* editor asked me to design three men's sweaters for an editorial spread and orders just flooded in. I launched my own line in 1985.

RIKA CONTOMPASIS

LOS ANGELES

Fashion is one of best professions I know for relating your creative and business sides.

Sport jacket in hand-
woven Bleached Wood
Stripe over fly front
linen shirt and
tickweave trousers.

VIC

Handwoven reversible
crewneck in a Floating
Boxes pattern.

TOR DE LA ROSA

BIANCULLI BY VICTOR DE LA ROSA, SAN FRANCISCO

begin my design process by first choosing a season's color palette. I then search out literally hundreds of threads and yarns in these colors, which will be handwoven into my own fabrics. These handwoven fabrics are the foundation for each of my collections. To them I add a range of fabrics from mills around the world to balance and complete the line. Whether solid or patterned, the mill fabrics must not only complement the handwovens, but also be exciting enough to stand alone.

Color is the most wonderful raw material I use. I want it to cast a mood over each of my pieces. An unexpected color mix or an unusual color accent can give a new spirit to even the most traditional item of menswear. A unique sense of color balance is one of the signatures of my collections. I feel most at home with a very complex, sophisticated palette in which I can continuously harmonize new colors in new ways. Since I design and weave most of my own fabrics, I can literally build my fabric yarn by yarn to achieve the exact balance of color, texture, and pattern that I need.

Texture is another very important element. While color brings excitement to clothing, texture gives it depth and luxury. By playing subtle shades of color off each other in my fabrics I can achieve a rich texture both tonally and three-dimensionally. Texture and pattern can exist even in a solid colored fabric. A solid white fabric, for instance, may be woven in a mixture of as many as thirty different fibers, from delicate silk yarn to ribbon to rayon tire cord. The fibers each have their own inherent texture, which when woven together into a single fabric create a pattern and texture that no single fiber can offer. By changing the mix of color and yarn, the texture of the fabric can go from subtle to bold, or anywhere in between.

Although my color choices are often inspired by nature, I've found over the years that my most original *design* choices come from the man-made world. Clean geometric shapes in modern architecture, primitive designs of antique African art, simple shapes of children's toys, or even an old brick walkway have all been sources of inspiration for me. I love translating the beauty I see in everyday things into fabric and clothing designs. Studying the work of some of our great architects has also given me a tremendous amount of inspiration. Michael Graves' bold, unexpected use of color and Kevin Roche's unique approach to proportion and line have given me the courage to inject exciting new ideas into my own work.

I was born in Oakland in 1958. Although I always loved art and color, my earliest career interests centered around more structured technical subjects such as architecture. It wasn't until college that I realized I could combine the artistic independence of art with the technical discipline of geometry. Even now, this dual interest is evident in the geometric quality of most of my fabrics, many of which I design on a computer screen rather than a sketch pad.

I originally went to UCLA to study art and costume design. The frustration of not being able to find just the right fabric that I envisioned for my costumes led me naturally into wanting to design the fabric as well. I transferred to the Art Department at San Francisco State University, where I studied textile design and technology.

My first job in the industry was weaving fabrics for the San Francisco women's wear company, Jeanne-Marc. In 1983 I decided to

Handwoven Stacked Pyramid dobby-weave V-neck.

Handwoven Log Cabin Lace crewneck with Streamers scarf.

Handwoven Citrus-pattern sweaters with Deco Dot camp shirt and sport shorts.

Variations on a theme. Doubleweave baseball jacket and sweaters in jeweltone brights against a backdrop of Bianculli's looms.

pursue my interest in menswear and formed Bianculli. While Bianculli was originally a joint venture, I became sole owner and designer in the fall of 1986.

I have lived in the Bay Area all my life. Much of my inspiration comes from city environments and architecture, so I am constantly inspired in my travels. Seeing the skylines of different cities and the mix of old and new architecture are probably the highpoints of my trips. Still, for me, the old cliche is true: there's no place like home. There is a quality of life in San Francisco that I've never found anywhere else. While it is certainly more difficult to design and produce a collection outside of the industry centers such as New York or Milan, the disadvantages are far outweighed by just being in Northern California.

Of all the fine arts, music is my greatest source of inspiration. Whether at home or in the studio, I am never without it. For all its beauty, music is based on an almost mathematical precision. Changing only one note can change a piece of music in the same way that changing one yarn or color can alter the feeling of a fabric.

What I love most about fashion is the creative process itself. Each season is another opportunity to create something new and different.

L E

love   working

with silk and cloth

which moves with life of its own.

I buy it all in white

and dye in color

A   D I T S O N

MILL VALLEY

moods I want to express

when I'm ready to create clothing.

Where my inspiration

comes from is as difficult

to put into words as

saying what it is like for me to be

standing in a circle of giant redwood

trees looking up. Or running

in ice cold waves of the ocean

with silver foam all around

or glorious rolling hills

against a most vivid blue

sky.

Most of my work is of
silk. I take advantage
of its fluidity, its drape,
and the way it catches
light.

Color gives me the ability to create despite the limitations of shape dictated by a fabric's properties.

From the beginning I gravitated to the quality and weight of Oriental silks.

Colors create endless
worlds of moods. I feel
like I'm bursting with
color combinations.

Only the mind limits
one's work. I can work
with the same materials
for years yet new ideas
keep popping up.
Design is endless.

The woman who buys
my clothes is comforta-
ble in London, Paris,
Rome, New York, and
Los Angeles.

ES GALANOS

ashion is a living art. It embodies ideals of good grace, flair, finesse, workmanship, and the timeless beauty of line and form. A garment can be as beautiful as a painting. And as with any fine art, the quality of construction is fundamental. A dress with classic balance and line made of beautiful fabric should last for a long time. The works of Balenciaga, Charles James, and Valentino are examples.

I have always liked working with silhouette, with long and lean dresses fitted close to the body. Many of my dresses are complexly constructed, yet I want them free of fussiness or gimmickry.

Most of the time I work directly on a mannequin. I won't stop working on a design until I'm certain it drapes perfectly. The fall of a fabric is as important as its quality. I often use a bias cut and materials like chiffon, whose workability and drape enable me to develop the proportions I'm after. I line my garments with soft silks so they'll feel as beautiful on the inside as they look on the outside.

Fine embroidery is always fashionable in luxury clothes. I love the design-within-a-design, three-dimensional effect of embroidery. Sometimes I get inspirations from just sitting at a table and pushing beads around. More often I'll drape fabric on a live model and allow the final design to emerge. Then the design is sketched and the pattern is chalked onto the separate pieces of the garment. These pieces are stretched on a frame and embroidered. Each bead is meticulously double threaded. Later the pieces are assembled and the dress draped on the model. A jacket alone can take three to four weeks. Line, cut, drape, seaming—everything must be perfect.

There are only a handful of people in America who can do this kind of fabrication. Mine were trained either in European workshops or in Hollywood film studios. I have a staff that I've assembled from France, Italy, Japan, South America, and the Middle East. Many have been with me two or three decades. They never take shortcuts. (I've brainwashed them!) I insist on doing things the right way, even if it's the long way. I keep my operation small enough so I can oversee every detail.

When I present my collections I emphasize the purity of the garment. Nearly every collection features a cape. Capes present the problem of a great expanse of fabric that must have perfect balance. Most of my collections have at least one black dress. A black dress reveals everything; hence it must be perfect.

I was born in Philadelphia in 1924. My father was a successful restauranteur and a talented but unfulfilled artist. I can remember wanting to design clothes from a very early age. At thirteen I won an award for designing a cheerleader's uniform.

I went to the Traphagen School of Design in New York for

❙ approach my fur
designs as exercises in
simplicity.

My greatest delight is in combining detailed workmanship with aesthetic ideals.

one year—dropping design courses but mastering draping and design construction. Design was just instinctive for me. I sold sketches to various Seventh Avenue manufacturers. In the 1940s I worked for Hattie Carnegie, but New York had little work available for yet another fledgling designer. I was invited to Hollywood by Lawrence Lesavoy, a wealthy New York entrepreneur. The purpose was to establish a couture house of which I was to be the designer, his wife the owner-directress. Due to unforeseen circumstances the project was abandoned.

I became a sketch artist for the designer Jean Louis of Columbia Pictures, but due to a long and devastating strike involving all the Hollywood studios I was forced to leave my job since I did not belong to the designers' and artists' union.

Mr. Lesavoy came to my rescue and provided me with a scholarship to attend the *Academie des Beaux-Arts* in Paris. I arrived there in 1947 at the age of twenty-three. However, I didn't enroll at the *Academie* but instead found work as an unpaid apprentice at Piguet, a famous *Maison Couture* at that time. It was at Piguet that my tastes and talents developed.

In a year I came back to Hollywood. Jean Louis showed my sketches to Rosalind Russell, who asked me to design her wardrobe for *Never Wave at a WAC*. I decided to do my own collection. Jean Louis helped arrange the financial backing. I opened in 1951 with a staff consisting of one French dressmaker. I went to New York with a collection totaling nine pieces. I came back to California with orders worth $400,000 and was on my way.

Using black and white
produces a clean look
in my spring
collections.

My hallmark is a
simple, clean, feminine
look for the woman on
the go.

NIS GOLDSMITH

LOS ANGELES

I am a New Yorker who transplanted West in 1967. I came into the fashion industry when I was very young. My father was a patternmaker and an uncle was president of the Jonathan Logan firm. I spent my summers pushing racks in New York's garment center, then went to the Fashion Institute of Technology as a textiles design major. I learned patternmaking, marking, grading—the technical areas of the industry. As a young man the last thing I thought I'd end up doing was designing dresses.

I came to California when Arpeja hired me to oversee their pattern department. That led to several more jobs—even at one time working with the Beatles-backed Apple Group designers. In 1972 I opened "Ma Chemise." My blouses were an instant hit. Success came so quickly I was booking my seasonal projections just ten days in advance.

The designs here capture the clean expression of feminine style that I emphasize. They are from my spring 1987 collection. Using black and white produces a clean look for spring. I use only natural fibers such as cotton, linen, silk, rayon. Comfort plays a large role in my selection of fabrics—soft laundered cottons, knits, silky textures. Good accessories blend into the garment; you notice bad accessories.

My designs are the end result of many influences. I am always aware of and looking for new inspirations. People in the street, films, theatre, art, and literature are all resources. From there the transition to silhouette is easy. At the moment I am fascinated with the American Southwest and the colors, culture, and style of the American Indians.

My wife, Gayla, and I have finished restoring our California Mission ranch-style home in the Hollywood Hills overlooking Los Angeles. Our home is a comforting retreat. Lifestyles in California are less hectic than in New York. I find them to be more conducive to creativity.

Fashion design is a fun way to make a living! Creatively expressing oneself and seeing the end result on attractive women is very satisfying. Still, it is a business accompanied by anxieties. There are constant, unpredictable variables. Everything has the potential to go wrong. I examine the feedback my buyers give me and interpret it to my own advantage.

My clothes are a response to the needs and lifestyles of the modern woman on the go. She is an intelligent, stylish woman determined to get the best value for her money. The quality of my work will remain long after the price is forgotten.

ANA

Hand-dyed cross tunic
and skirt.

Crossover tunic and
pleated hood.

Image from
collaborative abstract
video project with Jody
Gillerman.

grew up in a small Indiana town. My mother designed dresses before she was married. We had the most luxurious costume box a girl could imagine. It was filled with wonderful things left from her designing years—hammered silks, black lace, charmeuse stripes against black crepe georgette. I think that if an adult's profession somehow relates to his or her childhood play, it is right.

Oddly enough, I am a jeans-and-tee-shirt kind of person. I suppose that creating fabric by hand and designing one-of-a-kind garments satisfies my dress-up urges.

I studied art in college. Two classes were pivotal to me, ceramics and the history of Asian art. After college I tried to get a job. All I could find was a lousy receptionist/typing job at a publishing house. They hired me because I typed a good letter on a day when the presses broke down and everyone was frantic. Great job, I thought, for this I grew up?

LISA HEDSTROM

EMERYVILLE

So I saved every penny and bought a one-way ticket to Japan. I had exactly $200 when I arrived, but ended up living one of the best years of my life. I worked in a students' bar, taught English conversation to executives in several companies, and studied ceramics. I ended up traveling two years through Southeast Asia and India, and it was Asia that brought back my childhood love of textiles.

I came back to study textile dyeing. In 1975 I took a work-shop on Japanese *shibori* technique at Fiberworks in Berkeley. *Shibori* is a sophisticated tie-dye technique that requires considerable skill but offers tremendous possibilities for invention. I became hooked on *arashi* ("storm") *shibori*—a folk tradition now practiced by only one man in Japan. This process involves wrapping fabric around a pole, securing it with string, then compressing the fabric into minute folds. When the fabric is dyed, only the fabric surface takes the color; the part against the pole resists the dye.

I began to work in my studio, trying this and trying that. I somehow had to support my silk habit so I started making and selling scarves. It was the perfect way to pay for the apprenticeship I felt essential for a fine arts or crafts profession. I took my scarves to Sandra Sakata at Obiko in San Francisco, and she is still my main outlet.

I saw the possibilities of creating innovative pleats and textures using the *shibori* process. One particular pattern creates the ripples reminiscent of the designer Fortuny. He never revealed his technique and people presumed it to have been lost. Who knows, perhaps this is how he created his famous garments. I use a dozen different pleats in my work. Their textures have been compared with ripples, feathers, mushroom gills, seashells, and reptile skin.

Hand-dyed, tunic, bias
skirt, hand-pleated
cape.

Hand-dyed, hand-
pleated shawl of silk
crepe.

Color is my release as I work. Limited production clothing is frustratingly repetitious, so I immerse my thoughts in the colors I'm working with. When my color sensations are happy, so am I. I remember the thrill I experienced when I received my first box of crayons—sixty-four colors! I memorized all the color names. Now *there* was something I could understand!

I change my garment styles very slowly. They are almost a throwback to the couture tradition in the fineness of their construction and details. The one drawback of handmade clothing is that it is expensive and usually sold to well-to-do women. But sometimes I want to create something fast, simple, and cheap. Recently I've created a series of designs I refer to as "Video Wave Patterns." These resemble the fine zig-zag lines on TV. I have done some video art pieces in collaboration with Jody Gillerman that explore these techniques. I'm experimenting with tee shirts based on video images which in turn are based on my textiles. I call them "Head Storms," which is a play on words of my name and the meaning of *arashi*.

Hand-dyed, hand-pleated tunic and shirt of silk crepe and chinasilk.

Detail from hand-dyed silk.

Hand-dyed, hand-pleated vest over hand-dyed dress.

Keeping accessories
simple lets the fabric
make its point.

We love exciting the
customer. Our clothes
are a personal
dialogue between us.

JEANNE ALLEN

A N N E · M A R C

SAN FRANCISCO

always had a keen interest in fashion but never considered a career in the field. I grew up in an era in which home sewing was common. My mother was an excellent seamstress and hand-knitter. Consequently a great deal of time and consideration went into developing my own wardrobe. I always had beautiful clothes, but rarely purchased anything in a store until after I left home. All this helped me initially develop the skills I use in my work today.

I am still a bit surprised when I list my occupation as "designer." It was an unplanned career choice. It began when Marc and I were living in England. He was attending graduate school in fine art and I began putting together dresses and jackets made from vintage fabrics. The motivation was mainly pecuniary. There was no "dream." It was simply a practical matter of doing something to bring in money on a regular basis. We soon found ourselves involved in a full-time, full-speed-ahead business. We became "designers" when people began referring to us as such.

Marc and I had met in San Francisco. After four years in Europe we returned to the City on a visit. We showed the clothes we had been making to buyers at Joseph Magnin's and Saks. They ordered so much that we set up a workshop to fill the orders. More orders followed and the visit became a permanent stay. We've lived here since 1974 and would not consider moving from the Bay Area, even though we have been told many times that living in New York would be better for our business.

Most of our inspiration comes from fine art, graphic art, theatre, cinema, or dance. After we saw David Hockney's stage sets for *The Rake's Progress* we did an entire collection of fabrics based on his designs. Our most recent fabric collection is influenced by the Omega Workshop decorative art movement popular in England during the early part of this century.

I admire the Japanese designers. There is always poetry in their work, a moral stand that holds little interest for the American design community. I particularly admire the work of Yohji Yamamoto, and of Rei Kawakubo. Their textiles and shapes have both invention and integrity. Presently we spend about a third of the year in Japan.

We work so hard that our time off is devoted to balancing our lives. We swim, study Japanese, see lots of movies, and read lots of books. We live in Berkeley. Like most of our friends there we are obsessed with food—it is more an affliction than a hobby. We love it that there is no interest in fashion in Berkeley.

MARC GRANT

I chose these designs to show the range of feelings evoked by different colors and prints. Many conversations can come from

them—not coldly intellectual dialogues, but whimsy, fun, and hope.
The choice of colors and fabrics depends on the time of year, what
the wearer wants, and the occasion—camping, lunch, dreaming,
dining, shopping, learning, dancing, or flying.

A lot of our inspirations come from images we see in theatre, dance, and graphic art.

We design by working with the fabric first. That is Number One, then comes shape, then merchandising. We rework the designs together. We mix graphic prints and solids. Shapes must be simple and outline is very important.

Accessories are important to me. Shoes and earrings are not simply necessary, they are musts. I prefer to keep them simple and let the clothes do the rest. We build in waist interest and lots of detailed closings, so it's not necessary to buy anything else.

I've always drawn. I loved life-drawing classes, was always interested in the human form. I painted huge paintings (eight by ten feet!) when I was twelve and had my first one-man show at thirteen. My original academic interest was fine printing, which I now apply to fabric. I attended the La Jolla Museum of Contemporary Art, then the San Francisco Art Academy. I got a Bachelor of Fine Arts from San Francisco State University, then a Master of Fine Arts from the Brighton College of Art and Design in England.

I never decided to become a "fashion designer." I wanted to help Jeanne. She always knew what would sell. I always had an idea a minute. It's a volley, a relay between us. It is totally emotional.

Other art forms inspire me tremendously. I enjoy dance, music, and art, but usually I think of fabric first. Ideas come from the most unexpected places—spider webs, a frayed leaf, pottery. Every medium expands your experience. Inspiration comes when you can translate into your own words the ideas you absorb from the world around you.

K A

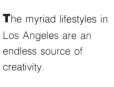he myriad lifestyles in Los Angeles are an endless source of creativity.

y designs usually start with a color. I then shop the fabric market or create my own fabric until I find the right mix for the season. Inspirations from around me give each piece its flair. Color, fabric, and texture must be attuned to the times. Climate is a key factor. Aside from the considerations of price, function, and timing, my instinct for natural fibers and colors is fundamental to my choice of pattern and fabric. Sometimes an accessory is a cherry on ice cream, other times it is a thread that binds the image.

Each collection evolves differently. I am never at rest, whether I'm working, at a play, by the pool, or walking on a path. I am always looking for new ideas. A button may inspire me. A tablecloth may inspire a collection. I wish I could say that every design and fabric was inspired by a deep-seated secret process that had no boundaries. But that isn't so. Karen Kane Company is a national and international corporation which must produce a line five seasons a year. Certain requirements are associated with that. I look for fabrics that match my customers' needs. I design to match an occasion.

R E N   K A N E

**KAREN KANE CO.,
LOS ANGELES**

I love fashion because I can see things blossom from a blank sheet of paper into a reality. But like any creative person, I'm frustrated when I rely on resources that don't fulfill their commitments. The one overriding quality my partner Lonnie and I have is our ability to listen, to accommodate. That doesn't mean we *do* everything we're told, but we take it into consideration.

I was a tomboy. To balance my interest in sports, my parents gave me dolls and clothes. My sister and I would make wardrobes for my dolls.

When I attended Dos Pueblos and Santa Barbara high schools I took all their sewing classes. My teacher inspired me to create my own designs and entered one of my coats in the Daughters of the American Revolution fashion contest. I won first place for California.

When I graduated from high school I moved to Los Angeles and went to the Fashion Institute of Design and Merchandising. At first I was interested only in patternmaking, not designing. I got a job with PHP industries. When their designer left the company, Lonnie Kane (who was then head of production and is now my husband and business partner) coaxed me into designing a few things. They sold well and I decided to continue.

I've lived in California since I was nine. I very much like California's climate and lifestyle. Lonnie is also from California and our families live here. The ingredients that make Los Angeles a great city—its weather, culture, freedom of lifestyles—are the roots of my versatility. It is almost impossible to feel restricted in Los Angeles.

All art forms reflect society. It is impossible for me to not be

Sometimes the quietest accessories give an image its distinctive voice.

Seasonal climate is one reason my designs are so varied.

influenced by art, music, and the communications industry. Other designers' works do not necessarily inspire me, although I do admire the work of Anne Klein and Calvin Klein.

I need change to rejuvenate myself. Travel is one thing that does that. I'm a people watcher. To see how others live, what they wear, and how they work inspires me. Lonnie and I travel for fabric buying and to oversee production, but it is more than business. What could be more relaxing than Venice, Italy? Whether unwinding on a ski slope or indulging in my hobby of collecting ornamental glass figurines, I take my energy and my world with me. I love where I'm going.

Pleated panelled coat: handpainted silk panels on black-figured silk, hand embroidery.

Pleated, belted, long coat ensemble: hand-painted, embroidered silk, antique closing.

J A N

ET KANEKO-LOO

**KANEKO,
LOS ANGELES**

Pleated jacket vest:
painted embroidered
gold threads on silk;
handwoven silk obi;
vintage Japanese
fabrics, antique
closing.

I am a California native and have lived in the Los Angeles area all my life. After graduating from UCLA with a degree in physical education, I longed to do more with my lifelong interest in art, so I went to Cal State in Los Angeles and got a minor in art in 1975. I tried ceramics, stained glass, enamelled jewelry—in fact, everything they had. I ended up teaching art for five years.

One day I discovered the art of the kimono. Their beauty, workmanship, handpainting, and embroidery struck me with a kind of inexpressible awe. There were patterns I had never seen before. Their color combinations were so unexpected and wonderful and the inner beauty of their subtleties was unlike any other art form I had studied.

I started collecting them at every swap meet, auction, antique store, and flea market in L.A. They might have seemed mundane, tattered, or unimportant to other people, but they were treasures to me. I used to bring them out at night after the kids were in bed and study/enjoy them (there was really no distinction between the two words), thinking of the hours, and above all the spirit, that must have gone into them.

Then I discovered a huge kimono resource from the most unexpected place—my mother. She had trunks of them in the garage; I never knew they were there. In Japan people don't like to wear old things, but they don't like to throw them away, either. So they store them in trunks. My mother's trunks were the collective history of generations of Kaneko kimonos. I was speechless.

Eventually I found myself sketching mental pictures of how they would look if cast into modern designs. I decided they should come out of the trunks and be seen, shown, and enjoyed by everyone—not in the form that I found them, but as kimonos reintroduced to our times in a different, contemporary way.

I studied each one, deciding how to cut or piece it together, whether to use full or partial designs, how to preserve the feeling of the original artist. I had to know each one in every detail—cloth, fabrication, art, philosophy—for they really were a summation of all of these. In changing them into modern garments I knew I had to respect the kimono's own spirit before my spirit could be put into them.

Cutting into the first one was the most carefully prepared event of my life. I literally took it apart stitch by stitch. Then I laid the pieces flat on the floor and stared at them, rearranging into new patterns and shapes. By adding pieces from other kimonos and obis some striking patterns began to emerge. Before long I was reassembling four or five garments into one. I began to use other types of vintage Japanese fabrics as well—hand-woven obis, silk obis, cotton workmen's clothing, sashes, scarves.

Pleated coat
ensemble: handwoven
silk obi, *shibori* tie-dyed
silk panels, vintage
Japanese fabrics, gold-
trimmed pleated jersey.

Pleated coat/vest
ensemble: silk
checkered obi, hand-
painted embroidered
silk, Japanese vintage
fabrics, handloomed
knit trim.

I knew right away that I wanted a more body-fitting Western look rather than the tubular Japanese look. Yet I wanted the shape of the garment to showcase the beauty of its fabrics rather than its tailoring per se. I began adding my own design touches—combining kimono patterns with black silk or knits, adding dozens of quarter-inch-wide pleats, emphasizing graphic designs rather than the cherry-blossom motifs popular in many kimonos.

But there were also practical problems. Some pieces had stains or holes in them that I had to figure out ways to turn into something useful. Some obis had been rewoven from older obis (in Japan, people too poor to buy a new obi reweave their old ones when they get ragged), and I had to take into account their greater fragility. And in a way I was involved in a race against time, as the sources for old kimonos are drying up and at some point the supply will be effectively nil. I'm interested only in handwoven, handpainted, and embroidered kimonos made of silk, cotton, linen, or ramie—which means I am necessarily looking for prewar pieces. After the war most kimonos were made of synthetics and the few handwoven pieces are expensive and of inferior design quality.

What started out as a hobby became a full-time business. My first pieces were sold on consignment in Los Angeles. Then Sandra Sakata at Obiko in San Francisco began to sell them, and through her I made a large sale to Bergdorf-Goodman's in New York. I stopped teaching to devote myself full-time to fashion. My little home workshop was soon outgrown, so I moved to a studio, which in turn was soon outgrown as well. Now my KANEKO shop in West Hollywood doubles as workshop and retail store. I have trained two women in the careful art of unstitching kimonos, and have two seamstresses to re-sew my designs.

But regardless of the success-story side of my work, what is important to me is that it is art, pure and simple. Fabric inspires me like marble did Michaelangelo. As I study each piece the *fabric* decides what it must be. It dictates the garment's color and design combinations as well as its style. I strive for garments which are lasting and classic.

P*leated coat/vest:* handwoven obi panels and pleated, hand-dyed, handwoven cottons; handloomed knit trim, antique closing.

P*leated coat:* black leather, handpainted silk, vintage Japanese fabric, antique closing.

Bold graphics on over-sized sweaters can highlight even the dreariest day.

I love finding unconventional ways to accomplish beautiful effects.

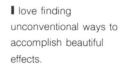

LES

A sense of daring combined with fine detail are vital.

feel that artists express themselves in many forms. Whether in steel, cloth, canvas, or stone, artistic statements are of passion and vision. My own sense of self-expression combines creativity with elegance in contemporary sportswear and knits.

I've always had a passion for fashion. But it was only while I was attending the Rhode Island School of Design that this became an artistic endeavor. All kinds of art designs found their way onto my fabrics. Eventually my clothing became an art form all its own.

Friends who liked my unique approach to fashion urged me to design a knits and sportswear collection. It sold immediately to the best stores in the U.S. Today my collections are carried by Neiman-Marcus, Lina Lee, and Lou Lattimore. Elizabeth Taylor and Joan Collins are fans of my work. My designs caught the eye of Norman Lear, who hired me as the costume designer for "All in the Family" and "Archie Bunker's Place." I also designed costumes for Francis Coppola's *One From The Heart* and the Hallmark Hall of Fame's "Aunt Mary."

LIE GAYLE KARTEN

LOS ANGELES

I am inspired by architecture in general and Michael Graves in particular. Draping, movement, the layering of geometric shapes, and attention to detail are vital to my aesthetic. I like to contrast subtle colors like charcoal and black with stark accents like mustard yellow and indigo purple. I love bold graphics splashed across oversized sweaters and dresses. My personal graphics signature is a burnt-orange leather square adorned with three gold studs.

I like convention-defying combinations. For example, the concept of rugged elegance will bring me to unite opposites such as rough leather shearling and chunky cotton knit with ladylike lace and opalescent buttons. I'll use multiple rows of antique buttons to encrust a bib or collar. Shapes that caress the body inspire me to accent with pleated suede inserts or a contrasting sleeve. Elaborate oversized sweaters can be adorned with leather, suede, and fur to create one-of-a-kind effects.

I come from New York and have an unabashed love affair with Manhattan (where I still maintain a design studio). I've expressed this in images of the Statue of Liberty in soft suede on a luxurious knit sweater. I created a fireworksy evening costume by putting a leather cutout of the Chrysler Building rising seductively up the back of a dress. I splashed the New York skyline across the back of a midnight blue sweater.

I feel these designs are perfectly suited for the modern woman whose clothing must be as inspired as her life. Fashion meets passion. I try to state that in everything I do.

I try to tattoo the body
without tattooing the
body.

R O

Ibo-styled longjohns
(front view).

am intrigued by the sculptural aspect of clothing design. When you put on a garment, a two-dimensional piece of fabric becomes a three-dimensional piece of sculpture.

My technique originated in a sketch I made of an appliquéd African dance costume. Then I found a book on Nuba scarification and body painting that really inspired me. Now I ransack old copies of *National Geographic* for images of the body painting of Amazonian Indians and Australian aborigines. I also collect tattoo patterns from around the world—the Marquesas Islands, Polynesia, Japan, America. I carve stamps from erasers and linoleum blocks into images based on Akan gold weights, decorated Nigerian calabashes, pre-Columbian stamps, manhole covers—anything that can be repeated or overlaid to form interesting patterns. I prefer to work on already constructed garments because I don't enjoy sewing. I am attracted to longjohns because the form is so humorous and I can create art on a second skin without the pain of tattooing. I begin with a lot of research but minimal planning. Usually some chance observation intrigues me; for example, the Egyptian collection at the Metropolitan Museum of Art inspired a mummy jumpsuit series. Once inspired, I go through my files and visit the library to find references on the subject. Then I cut the most interesting motifs into erasers and stencils. I use these to experiment with different patterns on tracing paper that I arrange on the stretched garment—my canvas.

Presently I'm working on an African series. What makes this series African isn't the pattern of the motifs, since they are archetypal patterns which cross many cultural boundaries and seem to be fundamental to all human psyche. Rather, the African quality lies in their color combinations and the structure of repeated patterns. I wonder if anyone has investigated the structures of visual pattern the same way linguists have studied sound pattern.

When I was three or four my mother bought me modeling clay. I created whole worlds of people, animals, furniture. Then I fantasized stories about them. By the sixth or seventh grade I was designing clothes. I drove my mother crazy because I didn't want to use patterns or follow directions. If I did use patterns I wanted to combine a sleeve from one and a neckline from another, or use fabrics that weren't recommended on the back of the pattern envelope. One time I practically destroyed her sewing machine by trying to sew pants out of leather. About this time the Summer of Love came along and everyone wore incredible costumes. My strongest fashion experience up to that time was six years in a school uniform.

In 1981 I received a California Arts Council grant that gave me time to develop my own art. At the time I was weaving large wall-

S E   K E L L Y

OAKLAND

Solar System shirt.

African Dance
costume (front view).

I am inspired by
archetypal patterns
which cross many
cultural boundaries.

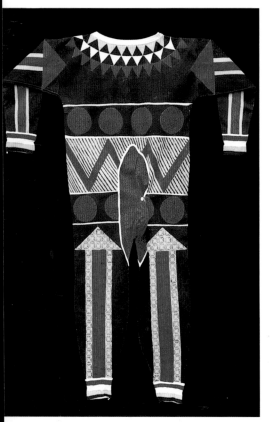

Heartline longjohns
(back view).

My images come from around the world—Africa, Australia, Polynesia, Japan, Egypt, the Americas.

hangings and coats and vests so elaborate I couldn't sew them on a machine. I came across an old sketch I had done of an African dance costume and it dawned on me that it was constructed like a pair of longjohns. I bought a few pairs and began experimenting with different dyes and pigments. A sales rep saw my work in the show, "Fiber, Fabric and Fashion: The Best of Bay Area Fashion Design," and started selling my work. I began exhibiting my work in art-to-wear fashion shows.

At U.C. Davis I met Lillian Elliot, who instilled in me the idea that textile design is not technique as much as it is being an artist—visualizing, trying, failing, learning from failure. Katherine Westphal taught me to use serendipity and humor in art. After graduating I moved to Oakland to study at Fiberworks. I bluffed my way into a job as a graphic artist but spent most of my time experimenting with different textile techniques.

Travel has been one of the most important schools of all. I became interested in folk art when I studied weaving in Guatemala at the age of nineteen. Guatemala is very magical. If there wasn't a civil war, I'd live in Antigua, the colonial capital, in a small house with a beautiful patio. Not long ago I traveled in Mexico, collecting folk art and studying Chiapan textiles. Most recently I spent three months as an artist in residence at Altos de Chavon in the Dominican Republic. Now I'm planning a trip to Spain and North Africa. I'm constantly reading about foreign lands and dreaming of when I can visit Fez or Kashmir or places where people wear clothing designs I can't even imagine.

Collaboration piece
with fabric artists Judith
& Lynn commissioned
by Sandra Sakata of
Obiko, San Francisco.

Our Lady of Rather
Deep Waters. Painted
silk coat with color
xerox transfers. The
shoulder piece is made
of painted hand-formed
expanding foam
plastic.

A K O Z E L

OAKLAND

design for the woman who takes pleasure in art and in vivid colors—a woman who understands that what she wears sculpts her. She sees in the power of beauty the power of herself. She knows how the right clothing unites body and psyche. She knows that if there's a competition for attention between herself and her garment, neither wins.

I begin with a specific garment in mind—kimono, jacket, chador, caftan. Each has its own configuration of shoulders, hems, sleeves. I am fascinated with the magic that happens when a static flat surface transmutes into a moving three-dimensional form. I think of the body as an armature on which fabric can be sculpted. Fashion differs from other sculpture in that fabric's softness and elasticity is constantly recomposed by movements as subtle as the air and as rough as running. My garments are sculpture for moving in, not looking at. Every motion is an inexhaustible variety of forms, so I never lack for something new despite the age-old absolutes of fabric, weave, color, and cut.

The cultural aspect of garments likewise fascinates me. I want to know why women have responded to certain forms for centuries. These forms and mythology—sea goddesses, fantasy creatures—inspire me.

I walk a tightrope spanning the art and commercial worlds, trying to pay the rent while keeping intact my own beliefs. I don't deal with seasons, with the fashion world, with press releases. I have a moral sense that I shouldn't try to fake it. The kimono, from which much of my work originated, is considered an art form in Japan. Each of my pieces, like the kimono, can take a month or more to make, yet during that time it receives all of me.

I derive my inner strength from transforming an uncompromising dye into a lyricism women can feel. My art depends on flow. Silk flows, the dye flows, my hand flows. When the garment is worn it flows around a body, at once revealing and hiding. My personality flows into the wearer's while retaining the uniqueness of each.

I start with "What if?", with a vague concept of the garment I want, then give myself plenty of "Why not?". Ninety-nine percent of my work is with crepe de chine. It has a tremendous drape. Crepe also takes color extremely well, and to me color is everything. I stretch the raw crepe like a hammock between two ropes. It is forced drum-tight with five to eight bamboo *shinshi* sticks. These pierce the selvage edges of the fabric and, like a violin bow, stretch it evenly in all directions. This keeps the surface more flexible and I can visualize the entire garment as I work.

My dyeing method is based on *roketsuzome,* a Japanese wax-resist technique. The design is created by brushing hot wax over

Working in Dallas in 1985 on an installation of suspended sculptures for the InterFirst Plaza atrium.

specific areas of the fabric so they will be "saved" from the painted-on dyes. Once you start dyeing you can't make a mistake. If the dye is down, it's *down*. The challenge comes in controlling the rigid inertia of wax and the watery flow of dye. There's a tremendous stress in this technique. Each dye has to be applied separately. I lay the wax over areas where I don't want color, let it cool, paint the colors on, let them dry, wax them over so I can do the next color, paint on that color, and so on. After a dozen or more rounds of this,

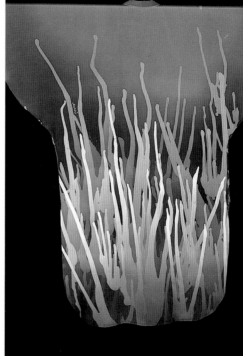

Nori robe.

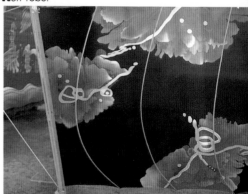

Bamboo *shinshi* sticks stretch the fabric outward as the dye and wax is applied to the other side.

From the Amber Kingdom.

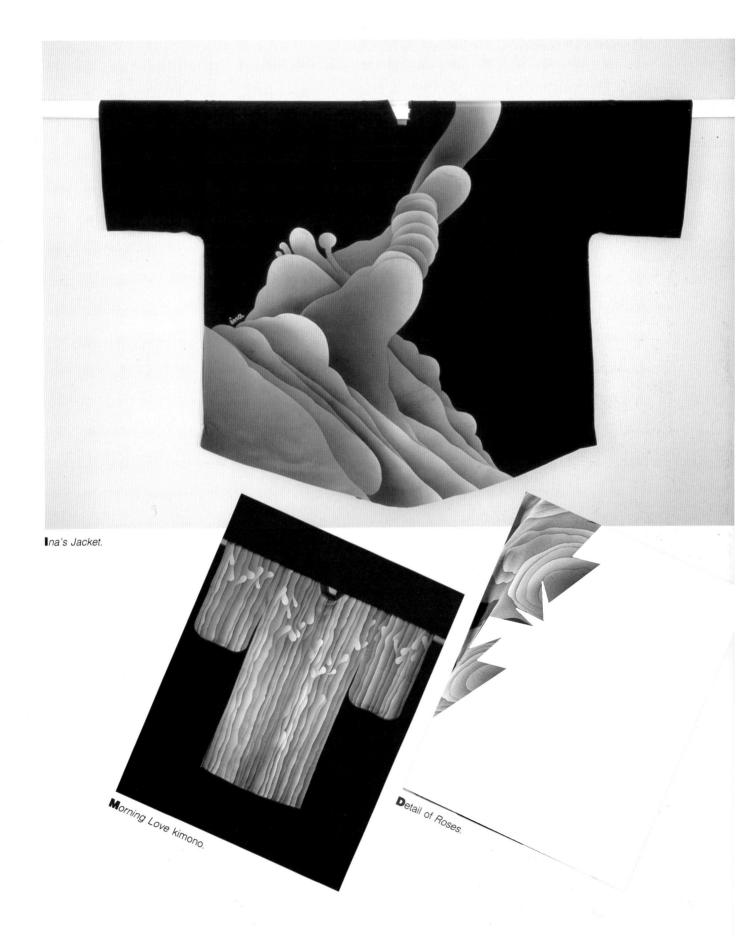

Ina's Jacket.

Morning Love kimono.

Detail of Roses.

I finally unhook the *shinshi* sticks and remove the wax by dry cleaning, steam the piece to set the dyes, and finally cut and seam the finished cloth into a kimono, chador, or whatever.

I was born in Lithuania and came to America when I was six. My parents spoke Lithuanian around the house, so I grew up with two languages and two ways of thinking.

I went to the Cleveland Institute of Art and Case Western Reserve University. After I graduated in the late 1960s I wanted to see the world from a very different point of view, so I went to India and Thailand. I stayed there a year learning batik. I came to respect the dyer's integration of his art into the society's cultural traditions.

By 1975 I wanted to learn more about the Japanese *yuzen* and stencil dyeing traditions. I went to Kyoto, where kimono dyeing is a thousand-year-old tradition. The kimono had an enormous impact on me. It combines unhesitating beauty, impeccable craft, and functional service in a garment so lovely it is timeless. Kyoto also taught

Detail of coloration technique.

Display at Rhinebeck (New York) Crafts Fair.

Untitled caftan.

*S*now Lake caftan.

*S*olar coat.

*D*ag's Coat.

me that an environment where art and artists are respected can be even more beneficial than techniques of art.

When I returned to California I gravitated to Monterey, which has the most Japan-like landscape in America. My work showed the effects of Monterey's mists, sea, sky, and treescapes in muted tones and meditative designs.

About eight years ago I moved to Oakland. The view was radically different—railroad tracks, abandoned industrial buildings, a scrapyard where car wrecks are turned into cubes. My work became bolder, less nature-like.

Oakland isn't exactly your lace doily environment. When people think of silk they think of mists on Japanese mountains or women on the Ganges. But I need hard-core Oakland to design in, a non-sissy environment so my silks don't become sissy.

FRA

NCESCA LEWIS

SAN FRANCISCO

am very attracted to the performance aspect of clothes, the fact that they are on interesting bodies doing interesting things. I enjoy subtlety and like to see clothes worn in a variety of ways. Design is a continual process of forming relationships between various elements. When they all work together the garment is interesting, comfortable, and versatile.

I take great pleasure in working with beautiful fabrics and then wearing what I've made. I've always made things, and the combination of art and function satisfies me more than any other aesthetic activity.

My design ideas come from all sorts of things—moods, architecture, music, dance, color, texture, fabrics. I also get ideas from watching people, seeing what they look like, what they do.

There's a practical side to fashion design that can be as stimulating as the more abstract influences. Practical considerations include who the garment is for, its cost, where it will be worn, and how to fabricate it.

Sometimes a design seems to pop out full blown and sometimes the process takes a great deal of effort. When I have problems with a design, either the design is not clear in my mind or there are technical problems with its fabric.

I've worked on projects as diverse as children's wear, accessories, costumes, and interior furnishings. I like exploration.

Purple leather coat; yellow silk jacquard blouse; hunter green wool gabardine skirt.

Black linen dress.

Black leather jacket;
black and white silk
jacquard shirt.

Pink and gray plaid
silk and linen coat;
gray striped wool coat;
gray wool gabardine
dress.

Pink silk jacquard
blouse; gray silk
jacquard skirt.

L I

L L I   A N N

JO SCHUMAN AND
JEANNE TAYLOR,
SAN FRANCISCO

Adolph and Jo Schuman.

Jeanne Taylor.

Lilli Ann is one of the oldest fashion firms in California. Adolph Schuman started Lilli Ann in 1934 with two secondhand sewing machines and two part-time operators in a twenty-by-thirty-foot room in San Francisco's Chinatown.

Today Jeanne Taylor and I continue Adolph's tradition in a 190,000-square-foot, two-building complex in San Francisco's Mission District. We have our own official Foreign Trade Zone designation to receive imported fabrics, and our own design rooms and manufacturing plant. Five hundred people work together virtually as a family and have been here twenty, thirty, even forty years.

Lilli Ann fashions are sold in twenty-five hundred specialty stores in the U.S. We have showrooms in New York, Chicago, Dallas, Miami, Los Angeles, Minneapolis, Portland, Louisville, Charlotte, Kansas City, and San Francisco.

We don't design Lilli Ann clothes to make newsprint headlines (although they do) but for the woman who wears them. *She's* the headline. We design for the active working woman. We want to create what makes her the most attractive. She loves the sun, the sea, nature, bringing the outside in. Hence 85 percent of our colors are brights. We have always believed that vividness and distinction make a woman feel more attractive. The man who appreciates this woman appreciates someone who has the courage to dress for herself.

While not inexpensive, our clothes are priced strictly on their cost sheet—and we keep those costs down. We sell two thousand or more garments in an average week, which testifies to American women's appreciation of quality and styling.

Our fabrics come from Europe, the Orient, and the U.S. They are the best available. We purchase Norwegian blue fox at the first auctions in Norway when the pick of the skins is available and when we can buy large furs of the best quality. Our designs use gabardines, flannels, machine and hand knits, ultrasuede, facille, polyesters, silks. Eighty percent of our woolens are bought domestically.

Our approach to color is to focus on one dominant hue accented with subtle coordinates. We order our color specifications directly from fabric mills—New York doesn't have the brights we like, especially for the fall collection. We don't follow European trends at all. Our production is based on five seasons a year composed of six to eight coordinated groups of eight or nine pieces each.

Lilli Ann mirrors the standards and fashion philosophy originally created by Adolph Schuman. He learned from his close friends, the couturiers Balenciaga and Chanel, and Carmel Snow, the editor who made *Harper's Bazaar* magazine, and who made Adolph her protégé.

From *Town and
Country*, August 1986.

His association with them began just after World War II,
when he was sent to France by the U.S. government as a consultant
with the Marshall Plan. Lilli Ann was by then a multimillion dollar
company and Adolph's expertise as a textile designer was needed to
rebuild the woolen mills of Normandy—a key part of France's econ-
omy. These led to other advisory positions with the Marshall Plan in
Italy and Austria. His work resulted in international awards and
accolades. He was given the Chevalier and Officer of the Legion
d'Honneur from France, the Italian Solidarity Star and Order of the
Legion of Merit, and the Austrian Olympic Order. Adolph died in
1985.

Lilli Ann's collections express today's newest fashion
directions, yet have the timeless classic quality that has always been
the Lilli Ann standard that Adolph created. They are the best of both
worlds—traditional classicism combined with a bold contemporary
look capturing a new generation of American women.

From our June 1986
brochure.

From *Vogue*,
June 1986.

Indian Feathers.

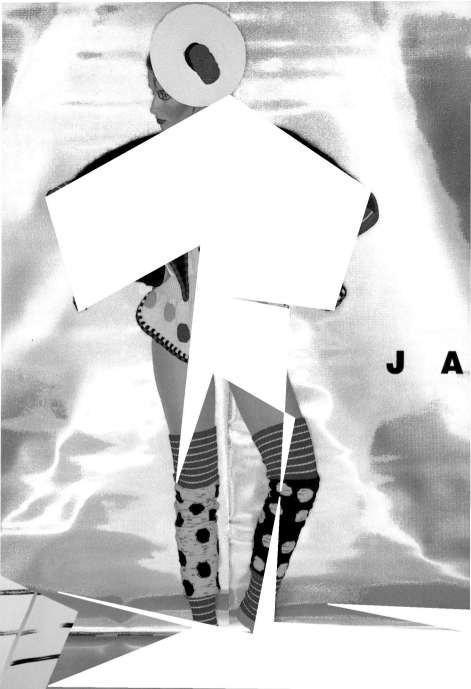

J A

Poc-Ka-Dot cape.

Kimono in Knots.

dith Head once said that if everyone was born knowing how to sew no one would need a therapist. If you could enhance yourself by altering your clothing you would always feel good about yourself. I agree. It is nothing short of magic to clothe a body and watch the garments come alive from the body's movement and life energy.

As a child I made paper dolls and paper clothing. I stored all my precious garments in my mother's china cabinet. About the age of ten I began sewing clothes for my dolls. I still have these dolls and I marvel at the detail in their clothes. I was surrounded by sewing. My mother and grandmother sewed constantly. One grandfather was a tailor, the other a shoemaker. It was in my blood. I guess I never had a chance.

N E T   L I P K I N

BERKELEY

I went to the Pratt Institute in New York to study fine art. There was a fashion department but I wanted nothing to do with it. Yet I was a very well dressed painter, wearing the layered, cut, sewn "rags" of the 1960s. My passion for garments was obvious. In 1968 Jean Cacicedo taught me the crochet chain stitch. I took off madly crocheting—inventing, creating, treating crochet as painting.

I started crocheting sculptures, but my natural direction became garments. I began to create painted crocheted vests. My premise was never fashion, always art. I saw the body as an exciting, moving canvas. In 1970 the first boutique to carry handmade items (D.D. Dominicks) opened in New York City. They purchased some of my early pieces. In 1971 I started working with Julie Schafler, who had turned her apartment into an art-to-wear shop. Two years later she opened the world's first art-to-wear gallery on Madison Avenue.

I came to California in 1972 and fell in love with the light, the color, the air, the creativity. It is natural to use bright colors here. They radiate through the Bay Area environment, inspiring me to create bright, luminous, humorous images.

In 1976 I was awarded a Fulbright to work and live a year in Ghana. I had always felt connected with African costumes. They are visualizations of the soul at one with spiritual life, as is my art.

I think of garments in terms of the magic of costume, of mask, the never-ending essence in all of us. I want my creations to live beyond time, to have a significance beyond trends in fashion and art. Each garment has a life of its own.

Colors are my true passion. I like exploring with their balance/imbalance, the shock of juxtaposing them. I dye my own colors so I can control (to a degree) the exact colors I want. I say "to a degree" because something special beyond my control invariably happens in the dye bath.

I often design in series—not a line or a collection in the fash-

Blue Leopard.

Detail from *Blue Leopard.*

Self-portrait in *Vertical Stripes* coat, a collaboration with Ana Lisa Hedstrom.

African Jacket.

Cow Coat, a collaboration with Ana Lisa Hedstrom.

ion merchandiser's sense because each garment is one of a kind. It's more like a series of artist's prints. Often a piece starts with a dream or daydream image, or something that catches my eye. My creative process begins freely but evolves into a technical dictionary.

I avoid the pressure of change for its own sake, the idea that things *should* be in and out of style. For thousands of years—and to this day in a vast majority of the world—people transform their unspoken feelings into something made tangible with garments. This is the realm of clothing that exists beyond what the eye sees. I sense it constantly in the dress of ritualistic cultures, in part because there is a sense of timeless human continuity in designs that evolve rather than being imposed. The power of a garment is its ability to transform the invisible self into a visible one. I want my designs to combine the body and the spirit.

Fur and painted jacket.

Painted leather bodice
from a collaboration
with Fumio Tanuma.

Painted cotton cape.

he sources of my designs are so varied it is difficult to sort out any single theme. They roughly divide into internal/external and organic/geometric. Just a few are spider webs, snail tracks, leaves, stones, sticks, ropes, eggs, the many different kinds of spirals, triangles, arrows, the moon, circles, crescents, snakes, dissected rectangles, fire, lumps, moving water, star patterns, bones, a cabbage cut in half, music, drums, whale songs. And on. The images I choose (or rather, that choose me) come from my state of mind at the time and could be considered autobiographical, a diary of what I am most deeply involved with at the moment.

The range of my work is as extensive as these images. Nothing is too small or too large to be considered an expression of wearable art. The smallest piece might be a single painted feather glued to a stickpin. The scale then moves up to gloves, bags, belts, hats, leather necklaces, feather collars, through vests, jackets, dresses, suits, and onward to all-endraping feathered capes and kimonos. But a piece's small size does not relegate it to the role of an accessory. I put so much of myself into each piece that it has an individual presence no matter what it accompanies.

LEE MANUEL

SANTA CRUZ

The work shown here spans ten years. It illustrates the basic materials I use: feathers, lamb suede, chamois, cotton, paints. I have to love the feel of the material I work with. My pieces must feel wonderful to me first; only then will they feel wonderful to the body of the wearer. Surprise is as important as substance. I'll sometimes use snakeskin inlays as textural relief to complicated surface designs. I leave sections of suede unpainted so its softness counterpoises the smooth metallic feel of painted surfaces.

What I love most about clothing design is form, construction, fantasy. For me the "fashion industry" is unimportant. I am frustrated by its resistance to even the tiniest of image risks, its incomprehension of a future beyond next season. It reminds me of Wall Street. Merchandisers cannot comprehend a gallery. Galleries cannot comprehend merchandisers.

I never "decided" to do clothing. I started with paintings on muslin that had holes cut in the middle so people could slip them over their heads. The rest has come from that.

I was born and raised in California. I went to UCLA and found the art department stifling and restrictive. I transferred to the San Francisco Art Institute with a promise to my parents to get a teaching credential (which I never did). The excitement of creativity, learning, free expression, and emphasis on making your *own* decisions was something I had never experienced before. The only negative thing that happened (which turned out to be positive in the long run)

Geometrics painted
chamois top.

Bent Sticks painted silk
kimono.

Bent Postcards purse.

was a trip to the San Francisco Museum of Modern Art, where we
were taken into the bowels of the museum and shown the storage
area. Fabulous works of art were shoved into slots to be resurrected
once every few years, and to minimal audiences at that. I was horri-
fied. To me the purpose of art was to show itself, to communicate,
not to be shut in in dark places. That was the beginning of what I've
come to be, even though it never was a conscious decision.

The only time I ever left California was when I was twenty-
three. I lived in the desert outside Phoenix for about nine months. I

still draw on the images I saw there and have visited other desert areas to revive the power of desert imagery. I have traveled to Japan and Yucatan and often draw from my impressions of these places. I have a tremendous desire to travel further and for longer periods of time. With paint and paper.

*C*athy's Dress painted blouse and Serpent jacket with painted culottes.

Lightning Dancer painted leather cape.

GEO

Guess? is fresh,
exciting, innovative,
and fun.

RGES MARCIANO

**GUESS?, INC.,
LOS ANGELES**

ince its inception, Guess? has always been, and still is, fresh, exciting, innovative, and most of all—fun! I attribute Guess?'s phenomenal success to the fact that my jeans maintain a forward image that is multidimensional. Men, women, and children alike want to be associated with Guess?. At the outset, my desire was to come to the U.S. and create an alluring image that would revive the failing jean market and create a staple in American fashion. So I introduced the overdyed "stone-washed" jean with an initial investment of $100,000 and a great deal of confidence.

Bloomingdales recognized the potential popularity of Guess? jeans when they bought twenty-four pair from me, which sold out the first day. Bloomingdales' customers loved the idea of a body-conscious, soft, comfortable, and fashionable jean. The next week Bloomingdales reordered three hundred pair and at that point I knew Guess? was to be a monumental success.

During our five-year history, keeping on top of the market has lent a hand in Guess?'s continued success. In addition to a diverse women's line, we've expanded to include men's and children's lines, and have recently introduced a knit line, all of which are doing well. But my strongest line is still women's wear, and since 1981 we have become the largest women's apparel company in Los Angeles, with 1986 sales expected to hit $230 million. I've also introduced other Guess? products to the market—Guess? watches, Guess? infant wear, Guess? hosiery, and Guess? sunglasses.

Another vital instrument in our success is our advertising campaign. My brother Paul creates a very strong image in keeping with the forefront of fashion advertising, using voluptuous, fresh-faced models who use little or no makeup for our women's lines. For our men's and children's campaigns, Paul uses real cowboys and children for a fresh look. Strong images and black-and-white photography add to the dramatic finish! Having been extremely successful in the U.S., we have branched out to European advertising, with surprisingly strong, positive reaction in England, Italy, and West Germany.

Finally, the flexibility that comes with working with family has certainly been a key to our success. My brothers Maurice, Armand, and Paul personally oversee with me every aspect of the business, meeting frequently to discuss problems and everyday business. It is with this teamwork that Guess? is kept operating smoothly.

For continued success, I'm keeping my commitment to my customers by offering new, innovative designs in denim and other workable fabrics to keep Guess? ahead of the competition.

One key to our
success is our
commitment to new,
innovative designs.

Our overdyed ''stone-washed'' denims helped to revive the American jean market.

J E S

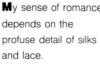

My sense of romance
depends on the
profuse detail of silks
and lace.

SICA McCLINTOCK

**JESSICA McCLINTOCK
FASHIONS,
SAN FRANCISCO**

y career chose *me*. I loved designing my own clothes and drawing patterns, even when I was very young. My grandmother was a patternmaker and a superb seamstress. Just being around her was my training in design.

I was always doing something unique with my clothes. As a cheerleader I wore short skirts before anybody else. I made my own tights in the mid-1940s because nobody else made them. All through school I'd sew things that were different, but I never thought about becoming a designer. I was raised to be practical, not waste anything, work hard, and follow through on what I'd started.

Those lessons must have sunk in because I was always a strong achiever. I studied ballet, I wanted to be a star, I fantasized about dreams coming true. I was too impatient to sit back and let somebody else set a trend. Now, I realize that's one of the prerequisites of making it in the fashion business.

I got married at nineteen and later moved to California. In 1963 my husband was killed in an auto accident. It was a difficult time. I returned to New England to teach. All through this, no matter what else happened, I was still sewing my own clothes. I found teaching wasn't for me, but I did learn how creative people need to make goals, set organization plans, and discipline themselves. Discipline kept me from flying off in all directions and getting lost in the forest of my own ideas.

I moved back to California. A friend told me of a woman who needed a designer for a small clothing business called Gunne Sax. I took one look at the sewing machines and one whiff of the smell of new fabrics and knew I'd found what I wanted to do. I ended up owning the Gunne Sax name. I brought to it my own concept of clothing based on romance—nostalgia created by a mixture of prints, ribbons, laces, muslin, and braids. It was late 1969, the "mini" era was ending, and the Gunne Sax "Country," "Edwardian," and "Prairie" era was beginning.

I did everything myself. I'd sell out one production and use the money to buy cloth for the next. I'd deliver cloth to seamstresses then go home and design garments for them. Production runs of twenty garments became fifty garments, and in about three months I was designing three or four collections and taking them to Joseph Magnin in San Francisco. I did everything—wrote my invoices, packed the garments, and delivered them. I never took anything for granted, and still don't.

Now I have a dozen showrooms around the country, computers, an ad department, and three hundred employees. I design about four thousand new garments a year. We ship to ten thousand

accounts, mostly in the U.S. I have to plan two full seasons ahead, keep track of the seasons in progress, and analyze what worked or did not work in seasons past.

I'm not a workaholic, but I put in similar hours. But fashion design is not work to me, it is my fun, my life. I'm up at six, at work by eight, break half an hour for lunch—usually at my desk to look at fashion magazines so I can keep my eye on what's happening—then spend the rest of the day in the workroom making sure my designs are going the way I want.

I do fifteen to twenty designs a day, which my assistants immediately fabricate. Sometimes they're perfect the way they are, other times they need to be reworked—a skirt needs to be revised or something else. I have three designers who help me as I revise, do swatches, make sure all the fabrics are ordered. When the fabrics come in I check them personally. We go through an enormous variety of materials—linens, silk jacquards, charmeuses, knits, appliqués, watercolor crepes, velvets, buttons, and miles of lace.

I have six lines at the moment—the original Gunne Sax (dressy clothes), which is my largest line, Scott McClintock dresses (contemporary), Scott McClintock sportswear (contemporary), Gunne Sax for Girls (dressy clothes for young girls), Jessica McClintock (designer collection), and finally Jessica McClintock Bridal.

Romance is classic; it never goes out of style.

A romantic design
must have good com-
position, aesthetics,
and visual abundance.

The days of California fashion as a romantic lifestyle carried over from the hippies have long been over. California designers are in an extremely complex business, but it is more fulfilling to work here than in other design centers because of the aesthetic beauty of the city. The hard-edge approach of the fashion business in New York is not as prevalant here.

Nevertheless, the California fashion industry is not a place for someone who isn't dedicated and talented, or who doesn't really *love* fashion design. Talent, excitement, innovation, and hard work are absolute musts in this business—as is picking out your market and concentrating on it. Most fashion companies that go bankrupt tried to be all things to all people.

I'm convinced that I'm still climbing toward my creative peak. I feel this peak will happen in my sixties or seventies. Your creative best comes with discipline, experience, and hard work. Work has been the longest love affair of my life.

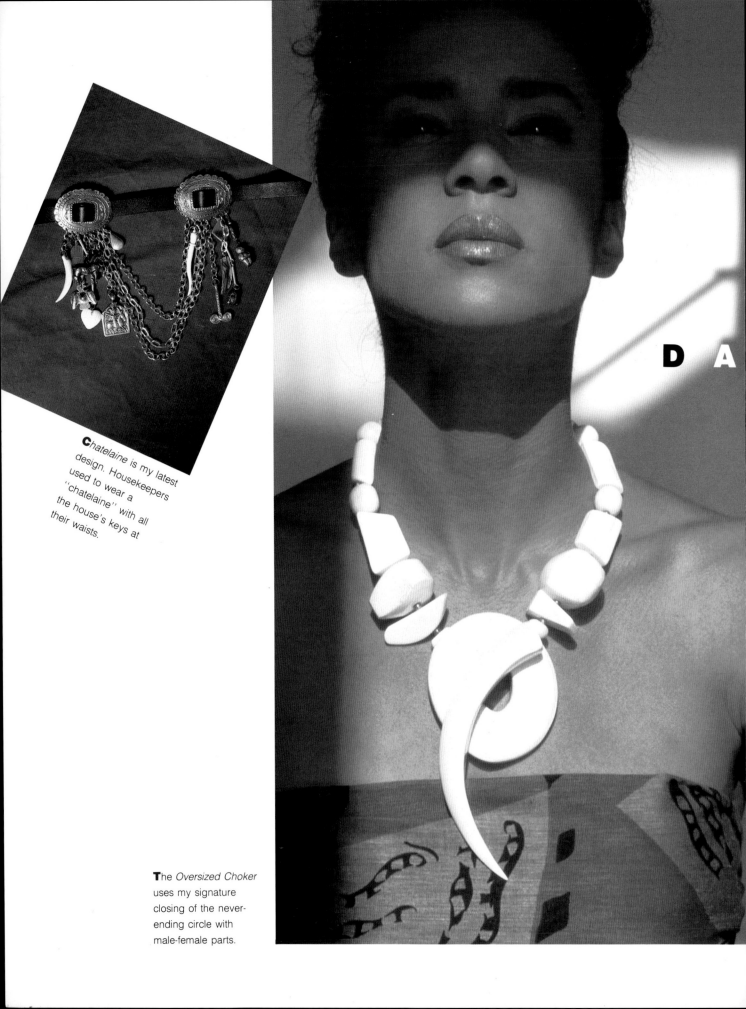

Chatelaine is my latest design. Housekeepers used to wear a "chatelaine" with all the house's keys at their waists.

The *Oversized Choker* uses my signature closing of the never-ending circle with male-female parts.

D A

VID NAVARRO

NAVARRO ALTERNATIVES, SAN FRANCISCO

When I was a child I lived in Palm Beach, Florida, in a Spanish-style home. I used to look up at the rough stucco ceiling and see shapes, and I'd make up stories to explain them. The shapes were always ambiguous, always appearing to be something other than what they really were, a never-ending story.

Making jewelry is like that. To get through the tedious beading I think of a story. I daydream. My pieces are narratives. Sometimes I think of a person, sometimes an event, and the piece shapes accordingly.

In the late 1960s I started an art deco shop in New York's East Village. I became a designer when I started creating pieces for my shop and people started buying more of my pieces than anything else. I began making "artifact" jewelery, incorporating charms, relics, and totems from all over the world.

Beverly Miller and I came to California in the mid-1970s. We left New York because of the violence there and because we didn't want to live and work in the same place all our lives. We came to San Francisco, fell in love with the city, and one month later we were in business.

The quality of San Francisco's light and its healthy environment are important to me. Space, at least by New York standards, is more affordable. In the East designers fixate on meeting deadlines and coming up with something new just to keep up with each other. In California, the emphasis is on perfecting your craft, not on going pell-mell and knocking out an all-new line every few months.

I take ideas from all around me. I'm greatly influenced by movies and even MTV. In 1975 Lina Wertmuller's *Swept Away* inspired specific necklace designs. The woman in the movie wore a gold chain slipknotted around her neck throughout the master-slave allegory. That chain inspired my "Swept Away" look—wrap-around necklaces with tassles onto which artifacts were attached.

Out of Africa reacquainted me with a woman of great strength, breeding, privilege, sensibility, and style. It greatly influenced my "African" look, not because of its art direction, but because of the elegance and strength of Karen Blixen.

I have been influenced especially by my travels to Japan, the Philippines, Hong Kong, and Italy. Japan has been especially important because of the Japanese sensibility and ideas of proportion, the importance of mixing materials, and the emphasis on the minimal. The smallest element can be the most important. Issey Miyake takes something primal, something that has existed a long time, and transforms it into a very modern piece. The chances Yohji Yamamoto takes in changing the body can turn the ordinary into something very

The Moving Choker. My signature closing for necklaces is a male-female circle and point.

The *Alternative* combines jade with fetishes, rare and antique silver beads, assorted lapidary, ceramic, cinnibar, and Peking glass beads.

modern; his sense of proportion is an inspiration. It's the same with Rei Kawakubo for Comme des Garcons.

Chanel gives me ideas for the same reason. My "Chatelaine" designs for this season derive from her use of chains. Harriet Selwyn from Los Angeles is another inspiration. She does classic, clean lines. Her designs grow. One thing leads to another. She makes a minimal statement, yet it is a build-up. You can layer her designs to create your own look.

When I create a piece, I essentially do everything in reverse. My materials dictate to me—I have to find specific uses for them. I don't start with a preconceived idea of what I am going to make. I try not to alter shapes, although any rule can be broken.

The *Alternative* pin symbolizes much of the philosophy of my work.

These belts are based on the Japanese *tsuba* (sword guard).

Gypsy Necklace incorporates a mix of oversized sterling charms, ivory netsuke, amethyst, turquoise, agate, and horn.

I first work out the mechanics of fabrication. Each part has to lay properly, but what are its stress points? How will I attach the component parts? How should I configure the closure? The oldest law of mechanics in jewelry is the circle, but I have to find the way through the never-ending circle to the point where its closure will be most simple because it is most natural.

I like natural colors. In nature we are bombarded with colors, yet no one color dominates. Hence I avoid stating a color in an obvious way. I build a color by suggestion. If I'm making a bone necklace I shade the bone with grays, greens, yellows, and browns. In doing silver I never use just silver. I shade the silver in my build-up with clear, pale blues, and sometimes throw in small copper hishi beads. If I do a purple necklace, I won't use only purple stones, I'll use grays, blues, even pinks, to suggest a purple, then accent it with lavender or purple stones.

I use stone, metal, wood, ivory, bone, glass, beads, and trinkets. I combine antique with contemporary pieces. I incorporate a wide variety of old and new charms—Egyptian, Tibetan, Chinese, African, Indian, Haitian, European, Catholic, Jewish, Arab, tribal, modern, and so on. Mystical, magical amulets, and talismans are constants in my work that underlie its continuing evolution. They are as old as humankind; I simply give them a new interpretation. Yet I also try to build a certain amount of shock in my work.

Polyurethane-coated
waterproof fabric from
France in a "Butterfly"
raincoat.

B A B

Handwoven jacket
trimmed in black
wool jersey to
match jersey dress.

Fuschia butterfly dress
of wool jersey.

he greatest direct influences on my work are the colors, shapes, textures, and proportions I find in architecture, industrial design, and graphic design. The most visible expressions of these are in my juxtapositions of colors and my choice of fabrics and accessories.

One of my signatures is the use of bright primary colors outlined in black. To me color is life, it is the elimination of ambiguities, it is boundless exhilaration. Yet it can be heightened if framed with black—the stronger the illusion of this frame, the stronger the identity of the garment.

The hallmarks of my style are bold, draping shapes, details such as black binding to outline edges, clear colors, and interesting closures like custom-made buttons and high-tech zippers.

E T T E   P I N S K Y

I also have a passion for blocking together three colors. My favorite contrasts are solids such as purple and black. Red and mint green used together are also high on the list, all used with undiluted, simple shapes. I think of these dresses as fragments of the architecture they will be seen in.

I'm fascinated with technically advanced fabrics originally developed for other industries and later adapted to clothing. In 1983 I made a raincoat with a translucent, coated upholstery fabric. That led me to create five successful collections of raincoats using similar coated fabrics.

Accessories can either harmonize or clash with the clean simplicity of my basic designs, hence their selection is crucial. I prefer to see jewelry employing very industrial-looking graphic designs—layered or starkly simple triangles, circles, and squares as earrings, for example. Bent plastic or metal as bracelets. Combinations of these as necklaces. Well-chosen gloves can be a godsend; they become a third color accent. I like to put tight hats on small-looking heads or use large brims for graphic strength.

My creative process is fairly straightforward. First I sketch ideas that have accumulated in my mind and in the notebooks I use every day. Then I cut flat patterns. At this point the idea in the sketch may disappear to be replaced by a new one inspired by the pattern pieces themselves. The pattern is then cut and sewn to create a toile or muslin. Most corrections to proportion and fit occur there. The revised pattern is then cut in the fabric I have chosen and the first sample sewn.

This design process is the part of fashion design I love most. But there's also excitement in seeing my work in a runway presentation and on people wearing it on the street.

I never wanted to do anything other than fashion design. In my teens I started working as a finisher for a costume company. I

**BABETTE,
SAN FRANCISCO**

graduated from the Fashion Institute of Technology in New York in 1962. They were very good at teaching fabrication skills but not very memorable as far as design was concerned. I wanted a total change of scene, so I worked designing raincoats in Denmark for a year.

Then I came to San Francisco. I designed raincoats and square-dance dresses for Malco Modes, where I learned about running a garment business. In four years I learned to deal with salespeople, sell, price garments, fix sewing machines, grade patterns, order for production, put a collection together, and generally run a fashion business.

Translucent laminated polyester raincoat.

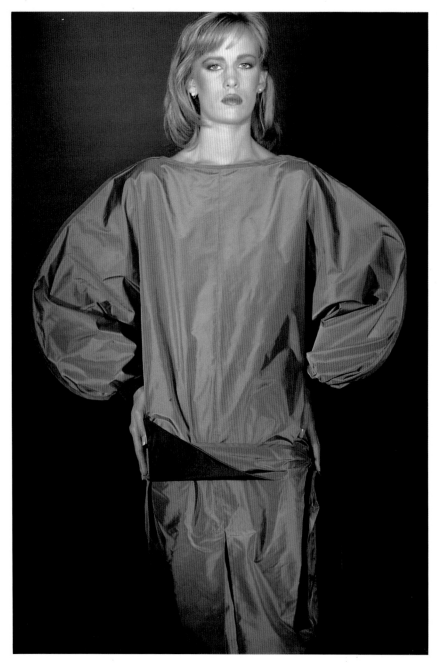

Wool jumper with geometric neckline and wool jersey blouse.

Silk taffeta dress trimmed in blue with black accent.

Mohair and wool jacket lined with silk organza over wool jersey hooded dress.

Double-face mohair and wool coat trimmed in wool jersey with a scarf through the collar.

I have lived in San Francisco most of my adult life. It is a city where one's intellectual and romantic sides can be nourished at the same time by the same forces. The exuberance of its architecture is a constant source of ideas.

Despite the fun and glitter of fashion, even in an environment like San Francisco, it is a world with its own set of problems. Money counts in more ways than you might think. One of my greatest frustrations is that I don't have surplus working capital to experiment as much as I would like before making the final decisions on a collection.

Today the fashion world is very small and ideas spread unbelievably fast. I feel the 1990s will see international recognition of the innovative fashions being designed in the Bay Area.

J I L

There always have
been, and always will
be, women who
demand flawless fabri-
cation in timeless
designs.

L RICHARDS

LOS ANGELES

design for the woman who dresses for glamour, who dresses for men. I delight in the current return to romanticism in dress, and to women's demand for flawless fabrication. A design should have soft drama. Nancy Reagan has become a symbol for this kind of fashion and she has been very good for my evening wear business. But the current emphases on romanticism and fabrication aren't new ideals for me; they've been my beliefs for the nearly twenty years I've been in business.

I insist that all my fabrics be of the highest quality. I often buy them overseas, although my manufacturing is done here in Los Angeles. My collections average sixty pieces, and almost always include pieces using my "signature" cloth, rayon matte jersey. I also make extensive use of chiffons, French laces, sequined laces, and silk jacquards. My ideal is to produce couture quality and style at below-couture prices—prices nearly every woman can afford.

I began my fashion career at an improbable time. In the late 1960s dressing up seemed to have become obsolete and tie-dyed tee shirts and blue jeans were the norm. I was having difficulty finding clothing I could be myself in, so I began to design my own. At that time my career direction was as an actress. I had considerable experience with Hollywood, but was growing disaffected with my acting career because I was so much at the mercy of whatever property came along.

We had a guest house behind my home in Beverly Hills. Some theatre friends and I turned one room into a design studio. Our first collection numbered, by my standards today, a miniscule sixteen pieces. But a friend of mine had a television fashion show called "Boutique" and he asked me to show my work. We showed six outfits. The *Los Angeles Times* picked up on the story and came out for an interview. The next thing I knew I was on the front cover of *California Apparel News*.

I realized that this was no time for stage fright. I took a long look at the ideas I had developed in my acting career. One of them was a sure feeling for the dramatic effects that bold colors can have on a personality. Another idea was the ability of a *little* razzle-dazzle to create flair without being pretentious—but watch out, the border-line is very subtle. Another idea was that well-designed clothes can be varied enormously to suit the wearer's personality, from a minimal statement to a powerful one in which character and costume become almost identical. Still another idea was how white near the face can be a powerful accent (another carryover from television). Hence you'll often see in my work a white collar or white detailwork such as lace near the face.

My approach is to give a woman every possible option. Every collection must have a design that works for her.

Theatrical principles appear throughout my work, allowing for considerable variations. The effect I desire most is a classic look which is instantly dressy and instantly glamorous. Hence I'll use fabrics which have a built-in allure—taffeta, silk, organza. I'll also make subtle variations that accommodate customers' sensibilities—if a shirred bustier shows a little too much décolletage for one person, I'll have a variation of it that's rather more shaded. She can also opt for the shirring at the midriff, or if that's not right, she can assemble a dropped-waist chemise with a shirred skirt.

The thing that inspires me most about fashion is the way it can be focused to bring out the best in a person's shape and personality. My approach is to give the wearer every possible option. She can always find a style that works for her, and I suspect that is why my lines have been so popular.

The design I like most is at once classic and glamorous.

Interpreting in black is
the most enjoyable
challenge I face.

O B

y creative process is usually inspired by fabric. When I conceive a season I start with the fabric I will use. I analyze my past season for styles that sold well. I consider these, the fabric, and my basic vision for the season. Then ideas just start pouring through my head, basically inspired by the fabric. Sometimes friends suggest variations that might work well, but my designs ultimately come from me.

I have always preferred black and white or bold primary shades such as red, royal blue, or purple. To me, life is bold colors, not muted shades. Pastels tire, they don't inspire.

I love natural fabrics. I prefer textured cloth, depending on the season. In autumn I'll often select a wool jersey. It seems flat but has a delicate texture. I'll interpret it in black, then add bold colors for accent.

ERTO ROBLEDO

SAN FRANCISCO

I create a line of thirty pieces six times a year— summer, fall I (transition), fall II (winter), holiday, resort-cruise, and spring. I usually concentrate more on spring and fall because they are the most important and the ones for which the stores buy most heavily. I feed on the pressure and competitiveness of fashion. In this business you have to be your best not just every season, but every day. You can't repeat yourself or you'll die.

We all have a market we try to reach. Mine is the sophisticated contemporary woman of twenty-five to forty-five. She is sure of herself and she loves good clothes. She always shops her market. But my work isn't for everyone. Some women won't look good in my designs, others won't like them. Thank God for that!

I was raised in Colombia until I was ten. In Colombia, women dress quite well. They buy their clothes in Europe or have them tailored. My grandmother loved to sew. I began to make Barbie Doll clothes for my sister from my grandmother's scraps.

We left for the United States in 1962. I was delighted with America. A whole new *country*—what a great thing for a young boy! We arrived in Miami on December 23rd, 1962. My Christmas present was a visit to a supermarket. I had never seen such a thing—in Colombia markets are outdoors. In the supermarket my parents told me to buy whatever I wanted. There were new fruits I had never seen—peaches, grapes, melons, watermelons. The best surprise was the door. I stepped on a black mat and the doors opened! I thought I'd broken something. This was modernization! This was a new life! It was the best Christmas present I could have had.

The inspiration to become a fashion designer came via a Merv Griffin show in which Halston appeared. I was in the tenth or eleventh grade. Halston showed his clothes and talked about his career. He showed me there was nothing wrong with a man designing women's clothes. I thought, "This is what I want to do with my life."

I love accenting a dark, bold primary color with subtle, eye-catching detail.

I began sketching. Fantasies of how women could dress flowed onto paper. Night after night, sketch after sketch, book after book. My room filled with notebooks, with cloth samples, with ideas. My father researched fashion schools all around the world. He learned of the reputation of New York's Fashion Institute of Technology, and I applied.

The first year I attended only part time because nonresident tuition was so expensive. I worked as an expediter for a textile printing factory. My job was to tell customers where their goods were and when they would get them. That gave me the chance to learn the intricacies of fabrics, of how they were made, how they draped, which designers preferred one weave over another.

I spent the next three years with my nose in a sketch pad, learning to be a designer in the heart-mind-and-soul sense of the term. FIT stresses the technology, the *process* of designing, from the ground up. Their teachers are very concerned that a designer should be able to take an idea and execute it from sketch to garment on the rack. We spent a good deal of time draping garments and pattern-making.

Bold colors bring out life's essence.

At the beginning I was in love with the idea of being famous and recognized in the fashion industry. I dedicated my life to learning as much design as I could. Then I discovered that design is within you. It is there so you can focus your talent on your work.

I love the pace and weather of San Francisco. I don't feel the pressure that I felt working in New York. I live and enjoy every day, where in New York I was just existing and not living. The air is pure here, and people are people. Although I take time off to get in the sun and the ocean, I live my work twenty-four hours a day, even when I'm on vacation.

Crinkle cotton plaid
jacket suit.

Silk tweed plaid blazer
suit with silk blouse.

P A

Linen blend jacquard
plaid evening suit.

U L   S C H N E L L

**ERNST STRAUSS,
LOS ANGELES**

was born in Los Angeles, where my father was a custom tailor to some of Hollywood's top stars. At the age of three I was taken to Copenhagen, where I lived until I was a young adult. I received my early training in tailoring and dressmaking at my father's cutting table, then went to the Danish Royal Academy of Fine Arts.

I eventually settled in Hollywood as an assistant to Don Loper. In 1962, I came to work for the couture and sportswear house Ernst Strauss. The firm is a rarity in the apparel world, a design-to-delivery manufacturer in which everyone involved knows each other. I can consult with production people if I want to know whether they can handle a design concept, and production people can come to me for last-minute changes if there's a manufacturing problem.

The hallmarks of quality clothing are fabric, fit, styling, and workmanship. Fabric is the backbone that unites a collection. The woman who cares about clothing can choose to be a polyester princess with closets full of mediocrity, or invest in a few garments of great distinction. My hallmark is uncluttered classicism. Color injects something happy into the closet and captures the spirit of the wearer. You look in a mirror to see your body, and look at your clothes to see your spirit. I avoid strict construction and the drabness of "three shades of gray" suits. I like to layer clothing lightly, the way men do.

Anything overly decorated or contrived smacks of poor taste. A feminine woman in clothes more feminine than she is redundant. It's so much better to reveal by way of concealing—after all, the most erogenous zone is the mind.

If a woman wants to buy only one suit that she will wear all year, there's only one fabric: silk. Silk takes color marvelously and tailors beautifully. Silk will last longer and go anywhere. It is also seasonless, which is particularly important in California. Because we have no true seasons, I use colors to create differences.

I start with fabrics from all over the world, searching, sampling, integrating textures and patterns and colors until a collection begins to take shape in my mind. I have always believed in pure fabrics—cashmere, camel's hair, wools, silks, and the twentieth century's pure fabric, ultrasuede.

Then I live with the fabrics. I let them talk to me. Once their color tonalities and moods have meshed, I begin to sketch. I do hundreds of sketches, in countless combinations, until something concrete emerges. Sketching is a frightening time. You have to create something from nothing.

Then comes draping, the choice of buttons and trims, the myriad details I have to consider before turning the designs over to the company's executives, who calculate time and cost factors and schedule production. My perfectionist details have to be realistically interpretable by workers, machines—and delivery dates.

My customer is a professional woman or the wife of a professional man. She has always been quality conscious, yet conservative in her clothing. She wants to look offhandedly chic, casual yet classic, like she doesn't pay too much attention to her dress, she just threw something together and it's absolutely great.

Designing establishment fashions in Southern California is quite a challenge. The sunny climate and casual lifestyles aren't the greatest stimulants for creating sophisticated clothes. The hectic pace of New York, Paris, and Rome, with their streets and restaurants filled with smartly dressed women, stimulates much better. But I feel Los Angeles's isolation forces me to look a little deeper into my artistic spirit. My work ends up being more uniquely colored and styled.

*T*hree-piece positive/negative silk print suit.

Silk/linen blend plaid jacket with linen print skirt and blouse.

Silk tweed plaid jacket
with silk pleated skirt.

Linen blend jacquard
plaid jacket with linen
print blouse and solid
skirt.

Silk tweed cardigan
skirt with silk blouse.

Nearly every collection
has something stated
in brilliant red.

P

YLLIS SUES

LOS ANGELES

I am originally from New York. Although I'd designed and made my own clothes since I was twelve, I didn't enter the fashion field until 1969, after a long career in the performing arts as a singer and dancer. The entertainment world gives you an appreciation for clothing that is natural, unrestricted, and free. I translate those ideas directly into loosely fitting dresses and skirts with shapes that have flair and drama.

Actually, fashion is very similar to show business. The work is very rigorous and there's tremendous emphasis on success. There's also a tradition that gimmicks don't work in the long run. You can't spend too much time worrying about stardom; worry takes all the joy out of the creative process. Everybody expects to bomb once in awhile.

When I left the East Coast I was influenced by New York's dark colors. It didn't take long for a major change to occur due to the West's light. Now white is my predominant color; I use black only as an accent. I also find that red pops up regularly in my collections. If I use a color that is not bright, you can be sure there will be surface interest in the fabric—perhaps shimmering dark or mixed with bright.

I've always liked fabrics with unusual texture and design, for which cotton, rayon, viscose, and silk work well. For myself I like cotton under everything and then layering with more cotton. My customers are used to this way of dressing twelve months a year. In this part of California there aren't any true seasons, but I find more and more people across the country considering seasons of little importance any more. The woman who wears my clothes can travel from one coast to the other without changing her wardrobe except to layer it for warmth or shed for coolness.

Women buy my clothes season after season because I give them interesting and unusual fabrications. It is a great challenge to find new fabrics and I depend on innovative mills all over the world. I often create my own fabrics by inventing techniques to change the surface look, or even by hand-painting.

My designs aren't for every woman—and certainly not for shrinking violets. My work appeals to someone who is sure of herself and who isn't afraid of unusual silhouettes. She is active, independent, intelligent. She wants to dress with ease and shift her wardrobe back and forth on a daily basis. I'm especially inventive with pants. I like to create them in unusual lengths and styles. I avoid trends as inherently self-canceling. I stayed with natural fibers when polyester was the rage and avoided the mini and the maxi tempests. My customers like to wear unique clothing but don't want to look like everyone else.

In the past five years there has been a great change in fashion—a change toward simplicity, simple shapes. This translates to excitement and fun being achieved through details. I think I am different in that my clothes are lighthearted yet the detail work is paramount. Fashion that takes itself seriously tends to be heavy-handed and even a little boring.

I am absolutely caught up in the excitement of this business and with owning my own company. I wouldn't change it for the world. The fascinating thing about fashion design is knowing you need newness each and every day yet not knowing what *kind* of new-ness your imagination will dream up. The other side of the coin is the constant anxiety (five times a year!) of a new line not being accepted, plus making the shipping dates for each collection.

The interesting thing about this business is that once you make it you can take yourself as far as you like. How large you let your business become is your own decision. That is an extremely emo-tional decision because if you do decide to become a tycoon you will lose the personal relationship with the designing side of the business. It's a decision I haven't been able to make yet. I thrive on the personal touch, not only with the design and business sides of my career, but with the customers and buyers as well.

White began to appear in my collec-tions almost as soon as I arrived in California.

The woman who is comfortable in unusual silhouettes has always inspired my work.

I delight in finding or designing fabrics that evoke unusual layered effects.

I am delighted this book came along. It is long overdue. I have spent a great deal of time encouraging young West Coast designers and building up the image of California as a fashion center. California is unique in the fashion world. Beginners can try out new ideas with no fashion establishment telling them they're wrong or that their styles won't make it in the marketplace. New York, Paris, and Milan are full of rules. In California, anything goes, and you don't have to fear being controversial or bucking the mainstream. Many people probably don't realize just how much Europe copies the California look, especially with casual wear. No matter where I go I find people who are in awe of California and especially the style of Los Angeles.

Spring 1987 Esprit
Accessories and
Shoes.

Spring 1987 Esprit
Collection.

Spring 1987 Esprit
Collection and Esprit
Kids.

IE TOMPKINS

**ESPRIT,
SAN FRANCISCO**

am not a fashion designer. I never made such a decision. I started as a bored housewife. I'd just returned from Europe with my friend Jane Tice and we couldn't get the clothes we wanted in the U.S.A. We learned to interpret the times in terms of what to wear. We watched people, learned what they wanted to say, and helped them interpret it. Fashion is body language and we supply the vocabulary.

I'm a second generation Californian. I've never thought of moving anywhere else. How could anyone think of living anywhere but San Francisco? Growing up in San Francisco was a social event. It was a rebellious experience. Getting smart without academic influence. Crashing deb parties and refusing to wear shoes to school. Formal education wasn't important to me. I graduated from high school in 1960. Wearing uniforms to school taught me to think for myself, to be an individual. I needed to stand out and wanted to personalize my uniform. I learned to alter the uniform to express my individuality.

When I want to get away from my work, I have a party, visit friends, travel to the South of France. Travel has been very important to me. I am more influenced by people on the street than the designs of recognized fashion designers. Everything influences me, particularly native things—doorways in Tunisia or old shop windows in China. Yet Norman Foster's building in Hong Kong is so important.

Life is art—how you see things, what you're interested in. I think people today want to nourish themselves. We're past the era of trends; the important words now are individuality, information, independent, introspective, inspired, intelligent. They all begin with "in" because people are really turning inward, recognizing their own value.

Today, people are too busy with their professions and with satisfying their curiosity to give priority to shopping. This seems to be why the look today is such a natural style, reflecting the individual's personality. Simplicity speaks for itself.

Spring 1987 Esprit Sport.

Spring 1987 Esprit
Collection.

Spring 1987 Esprit
Kids.

Spring *1987* Esprit
Collection.

Spring *1987* Esprit
Sport.

Spring *1987* Esprit
Collection.

Our *Clear/Frost* work is shaped from hot acrylic, twisted over the cording to create a floating effect.

Two of our heat-formed concave/convex signature pieces.

FRAN

ANNE VIGNERI

K AND ANNE VIGNERI

**VIGNERI, INC.,
OAKLAND**

Most of our jewelry is bought to go with specific garments, often for the seasonal releases around the world. We have to keep a sharp eye on fashion trends so our color choices will work with the greatest possible cross section of garments in stores. What we have to watch out for is a strong line using olive green when forest green is the next color trend.

Our "fabric" is acrylic combined with lacquer, gold, and sterling. We use unusual surfaces and innovative fabrications to interpret plastics in new ways. People tell us we *can't* do what we do. That's why we love acrylic so much. It can be carved, incised, inlaid, bent, heated, warped, mashed, abraded, pierced and all sorts of other dreadful-sounding things. But only by constant experimentation, by breaking the "rules" in improbable ways, have we made our best discoveries.

Our process begins with shapes, shapes, and more shapes. Frank is constantly drawing ideas and impressions, forms, and the ways shape enhances the body or face. Sketch pads are all over the house, the car, the studio. When we travel, they're all over hotel rooms and restaurant tables.

Then we look at his themes and a few winners pop out. Recently we were inspired by pre-Columbian art. We've also done some very successful designs based on Bauhaus motifs. When San Francisco's de Young Museum hosted an exhibition of Japanese samurai helmets we were taken by their colors and the way their designs combined the functional with the artistic.

I bet a lot of designers started the way I did. As a child I loved "dressing up." I'd take old table cloths and curtains and wrap myself into what I was certain was the most elegant thing on the planet. I always made an effort to look "different." Sometimes it backfired. When I was in high school I bought a little girl's skirt that came above my knees and wore it over matching tights from a ballet school. I wore this to school and was sent home to change into "appropriate attire." From that day forward I've been trendsetting.

After graduating from high school (in appropriate attire) I attended some "modeling" schools. These dispensed some highly sophisticated B.S. which landed few jobs. I decided I had enough confidence in my taste to rely on it for a living. I still have no formal fashion education beyond doing it.

FRANK VIGNERI

I have very vivid and happy memories of being in the first grade and being chosen for a museum exhibit of sculpture by school children. My clay soldier was a hit!

My early sketches and models impressed my peers. They loved my gliders, ice boats, motorbikes. My family moved a lot. Perhaps constant adaptations influenced my creative side. In college I took as many painting and sculpture courses as I could. My teachers encouraged me to move in the direction of their art but to *re*move my favorite work—a twelve-by-five-foot painted canvas I'd formed into a cylinder. Art-in-the-round was a little unorthodox for them.

I came to Los Angeles. I was invited to the house of a fellow artist. Five minutes later I met Anne. She walked into his apartment, looked me over, and said, "Let's go to the beach." We spent the day sculpting sand. By the end of the day our first exhibition was a success. Unhappily, no reviewers from the major papers were present.

By 1982 we had a modest jewelry business. A client came by to look some over. Anne was working on one of our experimental jewelry pieces. The woman took one look and said imperiously, "Prepare yourself for a phone call." Sure enough, the next day a Macy's buyer called and wanted to see our "line." We didn't know

Hand-carved acrylic formed from flat sheets.

The most complex cast polyesters we've ever done.

Individually shaped acrylic petals on a collar of hand-knotted gold and black ribbons.

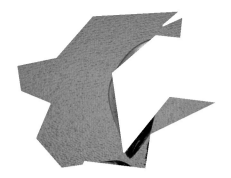

Bracelets are shaped after a carved blank has been heated in an oven.

An interpretation of an ancient bone necklace using modern materials.

what a line *was!* The woman was the wife of a Macy's president and when she spoke, mere mortals trembled. A short time later a friend took one of our pieces to a buyer for Saks Fifth Avenue. Saks had a policy that all buying had to be done through New York. But their buyer said she was going to go out on a limb and buy several thousand dollars' worth of our things, and if she was wrong, she'd be out of a job. She still has her job and we're still selling to Saks. Not long after *that* Anne was shopping in Britex and she heard a voice she recognized. She couldn't place the face, though, so she introduced herself. It turned out that the voice belonged to an old high-school friend, who happened to work for George Lucas. The next thing we knew, twenty of our pieces showed up in *Return of the Jedi.*

We have a wonderful big old house with a garden and love to spend hours outside looking at the sky, the redwood tree, the flowers. We unwind by eating in some of the Bay Area's best restaurants. In 1974 we started making homemade wine with friends and have won a tidy number of awards in local competitions. So far Ernest and Julio Gallo haven't anything to worry about, but you never know, this is California.

California! It's the good life, absolutely. We have a workplace we could never afford in New York. We can walk two blocks to San Francisco Bay, watch sailboats go by, eat oysters, and drink champagne (*California* champagne!). I could recommend a few brands, but want to wait until we've made our own. You never know.

K A

Inspired by the incredible formation of the human body, I realized that even without training I had a special talent for graphic arts. I found inspiration within.

My work is an attempt to recapture

SIK WONG

SAN FRANCISCO

Paradise Lost. My vision of Eden inspires me to create what people might wear there.

People buy clothes to strengthen their auras, the majesty of the body's chemistry and structure.

Amphora.

I graduated with a training in the basics of fashion design from the Pacific Fashion Institute in my primitive years, 1965 through 1967. I traveled to the East Coast and abroad, where I gained training in the actual work of a designer.

Creative.

Aramma.

Eden Mai.

Eucalyptus.

My creations come from a deep

inner unity by way of dreams

and visualizations. These creations

unite my immediate environments

with art forms.

*S*even Rays.

*R*ain.

I am a native San Franciscan.

The multicultural environment

is conducive to my inner being.

In my travels I seek the metaphysical

history of the continents. My

major influence is the remembrance

of El Dorado, Atlantis, and Lumeria.

My metaphysical search is for

the manifestations of my Inner Being.

When I find them I will have united

heart, mind, and soul. Answers are

eternal and omnipresent. Life is

eternal.

Plumeria.

Harvest.

WHERE TO FIND THE FASHIONS OF THE DESIGNERS IN THIS BOOK

The work of many California designers can be found in major retail stores around the United States. Other designers are represented by only a few stores, and a few can be reached only at their shops. You can write the designers in this book at the following addresses and ask where you can find their work.

JOSEPH ABBATI
Saxon Men's Wear
1931 Mason Street
SAN FRANCISCO, CA 94133
415-863-7709

KAREN ALEXANDER
Shady Grove
5601 San Leandro
OAKLAND, CA 94621
415-532-8400

GAZA BOWEN
130 Baldwin
SANTA CRUZ, CA 95065
408-458-1184

LAUREL BURCH
410 Townsend Street
SAN FRANCISCO, CA 94107
415-541-0400

JEAN CACICEDO
1842 San Antonio Avenue
BERKELEY, CA 94707
415-549-2251

ELETRA CASADEI
110 East Ninth Street
Suite C-343
LOS ANGELES, CA 90079
213-624-4996

MICHAEL CASEY
2325 Third Street #337
SAN FRANCISCO, CA 94107
415-431-9550

MARIAN CLAYDEN
16231 Deodar Lane
LOS GATOS, CA 95030
408-354-4747

MARIKA CONTOMPASIS
846 South Broadway
Suite 600
LOS ANGELES, CA 90014
213-624-2960

VICTOR DE LA ROSA
Bianculli
2565 Third Street #313
SAN FRANCISCO, CA 94107
415-648-6546

LEA DITSON
10 Woodbine
MILL VALLEY, CA 94941
415-383-3478

JAMES GALANOS
2254 South Sepulveda Blvd.
LOS ANGELES, CA 90064
213-272-1445

DENNIS GOLDSMITH
2807 Olive Street
LOS ANGELES, CA 90047
213-746-1320

ANA LISA HEDSTROM
1420 Forty-fifth Street
EMERYVILLE, CA 94608·
415-654-4109

JEANNE-MARC
Jeanne Allen and Marc Grant
550 Third Street
SAN FRANCISCO, CA 94107
415-543-5414

KAREN KANE
929 South Broadway #712
LOS ANGELES, CA 90015
213-622-6422

JANET KANEKO-LOO
618½ North Doheny Drive
LOS ANGELES, CA 90069
213-274-4096

LESLIE GAYLE KARTEN
1158 Greenacre Avenue
LOS ANGELES, CA 90046
213-874-4073

ROSE KELLY
P.O. Box 1696
ROSS, CA 94957

INA KOZEL
4701 San Leandro Street
OAKLAND, CA 94601
415-533-0781

FRANCESCA LEWIS
4508 Nineteenth Street
SAN FRANCISCO, CA 94114
415-626-5140

LILLI ANN
Jo Schuman and Jeanne Taylor
2701 Sixteenth Street
SAN FRANCISCO, CA 94103
415-863-2720

JANET LIPKIN
1153 Camelia
BERKELEY, CA 94702
415-526-0877

K.LEE MANUEL
139 Bohnen Road
SANTA CRUZ, CA 95065
408-427-0130

GEORGES MARCIANO
Guess?, Inc.
1714 South Maple Street
LOS ANGELES, CA 90015
213-688-7322

JESSICA McCLINTOCK
1400 Sixteenth Street
SAN FRANCISCO, CA 94103
415-495-3030

DAVID NAVARRO
2415 Third Street #263
SAN FRANCISCO, CA 94107
415-431-1346

BABETTE PINSKY
2343 Third Street
Suite 230
SAN FRANCISCO, CA 94107
415-621-2343

JILL RICHARDS
719 Los Angeles
LOS ANGELES, CA 90014
213-489-1650

ROBERTO ROBLEDO
520 Haight Street
SAN FRANCISCO, CA 94117
415-621-2502

PAUL SCHNELL
Ernst Strauss
714 Los Angeles
LOS ANGELES, CA 90014
213-623-8112

PHYLLIS SUES
1031 South Broadway
LOS ANGELES, CA 90015
213-747-7206

SUSIE TOMPKINS
Esprit
900 Minnesota Street
SAN FRANCISCO, CA 94107
415-648-6900

FRANK AND ANNE VIGNERI
208 Madison
OAKLAND, CA 94607
415-452-1066

KAISIK WONG
1234-A Jackson Street
SAN FRANCISCO, CA 94108
415-885-3111

PHOTO AND MODEL CREDITS (AS SUPPLIED)

Page

4-7 photos: Jeffery Newbury, model: Todd Mobley

16 (top) photo: Mark Rice; (bottom) photo: Lenny Lind

17 photo: Steve Fukuda

18 photos: Mark Rice

19 photos: Steve Fukuda

20 (left) photo: Mark Rice; (right) photo: Steve Fukuda

21 (top left) photo: Lenny Lind; (bottom left) photo: Mark Rice; (right) photo: Steve Fukuda

22 (left) photo: David Leach, model: Andy; (right) photo: David Leach, model: Sidney

23 photo: David Leach

24 photo: David Leach, model: Udette

25 (top left) photo: David Leach; (bottom left) photo: David Leach, model: Karen; (right) photo: David Leach, model: Andy

26 (left) photo: David Leach, model: Kennedy; (top right) photo: David Leach; (bottom right) photo: David Leach, model: Udette

27 (top) photo: David Leach, model: Jeannie; (bottom) photo: David Leach, model: Diane

28-31 photos: courtesy Janet Orsi Public Relations

32-35 photos: courtesy Alan Purcell

40-41 photos: courtesy Janet Orsi Public Relations

46 photo: Kaisik Wong, model: Jeri

48 (left) photo: Kaisik Wong, model: Jeri; (right) photo: Clinton Davis

49 (top left) photo: Clinton Davis, model: Kim; (bottom left) photo: Brad Mullin; (right) photo: Clinton Davis, model: Kim

50 (left) photo: Mike Russ; (right) photo: Helmut Newton, courtesy Xavier Moreau, New York

51 photo: Skrebneski

52 (left) photo: Mike Russ; (right) photo: Helmut Newton, courtesy Xavier Moreau, New York

53 (top left and right) photos: Helmut Newton, courtesy Xavier Moreau, New York; (bottom) photo: Mike Russ

54-55 photos: courtesy Luc Ekstein

56 (top left) photo: Barry Shapiro, model: Deborah Day; (top right) photo: Brad Mollath, model: Deborah Day

58 (left) photo: Craig Morey, model: Jeane Somers; (right) photo: Barry Shapiro, model: Barbara Irving

59 (top) photo: Craig Morey, model: Jeane Somers; (bottom right) photo: David Leach, model: Lynwen Jones

72-73 photos: courtesy Janet Orsi Public Relations

74 (left) photo: Earle Fox, models: Kristie Johnson, Richard de Marcos, Jody Stevens, Adele Fox; (right) photo: Rose Kelly

75 photo: Perry Johnson

76 (top left, bottom left, top right) photos: Rose Kelly; (bottom right) photo: Earle Fox, models: Kristie Johnson, Richard de Marcos, Jody Stevens, Adele Fox, Rose Kelly

77 (top) photo: Earle Fox, model: Richard de Marcos; (bottom) photo: Earle Fox, models: Kristie Johnson, Richard de Marcos, Jody Stevens, Adele Fox, Rose Kelly

78 (left) photo: Ina Kozel, model: Zhenne

80 (left) photo: Tom O'Neil, model: Rima Kozel

81 (top) photo: Gordi Yalda; (bottom right) photo: Ina Kozel

82 (bottom right) photo: Paul Herzoff, model: Diane

83 (top and bottom left) photos: Gordi Yalda; (right) photo: Dagmar Figl

84-87 photos: John Edwards, styling and accessories: Paul Butler, models: Jill Cristina, Anita Lassen, Melissa

92 (top left) photo: Barry Shapiro, model: Deborah Day; (bottom left) photo: Barry Shapiro, model: Sherri Hill; (right) photo: Barry Shapiro

93 photo: Barry Shapiro
94 (left) photo: Barry Shapiro, model: Annette Haven; (bottom right) photo: Barry Shapiro, model: Janet Lipkin
95 (left) photo: Barry Shapiro, model: Sherri Hill; (right) photo: Barry Shapiro, model: Lani Hoge
96 (left) photo: Barry Shapiro; (top and bottom right) photo: Lars Speyer
97 photo: Ed Clay
98 photos: Lars Speyer
99 (left) photo: Lars Speyer; (right) photo: Barry Shapiro
100 (left) photo: Wayne Maser, model: Estelle LeFebure; (right) photo: Wayne Maser, model: Christine Bolster
102 (left) photo: Wayne Maser, model: Christine Bolster; (right) photo: Wayne Maser, model: Estelle LeFebure
103 (top left) photo: Wayne Maser, model: Jo Kelly; (bottom left) photo: Wayne Maser, models: Estelle LeFebure and Cody Hanes; (right) photo: Wayne Maser, models: Estelle LeFebure and Frederique Van Der Wall
108-11 photos: Paul Cruz
112 (left) photo: Phil Saltonstal, model: Kim Brittian; (top right) photo: Kent Marshall, model: Charlotte Caldwell; (bottom right) photo: Phil Saltonstal, model: Kim Brittian
113 photo: Jeff Newbury, model: Jennifer Inez
114 (left) photo: Paul Cruz, model: Tansie; (top right) photo: Kent Marshall, model: Charlotte Caldwell; (bottom right) photo: Paul Cruz, model: Ethel Fong
115 (left) photo: Mark Farbin, model: Shoshana; (right) photo: Paul Cruz, model: Ethel Fong
116-19 photos: courtesy Janet Orsi Public Relations

120 (left) photo: Alan Purcell, models: Veronica and Richard; (right) photo: Alan Purcell
121 photo: Deborah Roan
122 (left) photo: Alan Purcell; (top right) photo: Maria Robledo, model: Mieghan Leibert, backdrop: Carrino; (bottom right) photo: Alan Purcell
123 (left) photo: Alan Purcell, model: Nicole; (right) photo: Leslie Hirsch, model: Anita Jones
124-27 photos: Dominick, model: Lauren Helm
128-31 photos: David Gray
132 (left) photo: Oliviero Toscani; (top right) photo: Roberto Carra; (bottom right) photo: Oliviero Toscani
133 (bottom) photo: Oliviero Toscani
134-35 photos: Oliviero Toscani
136 (left) photo: Brad Mollath; (right) photo: Brad Mollath, model: Kimberly
137 photo: Brad Mollath
138 photos: Brad Mollath
139 photos: Brad Mollath, model: Glenna Marshall
140 photo: Kaisik Wong, model: Shoshana
141 photo: Kailey Wong
142 (left) photo: Kaisik Wong, model: Merle Bulato; (top) photo: Howard Steinman, model: Kaisik Wong; (bottom right) photo: Kaisik Wong, model: Merle Bulato
143 (left) photo: Kaisik Wong, model: Shoshana; (right) photo: Kaisik Wong, model: Merle Bulato
144 (left) photo: Kaisik Wong, model: Merle Bulato; (top right) photo: Kaisik Wong, model: Merle Bulato; (bottom right) photo: Kaisik Wong, model: Phyllis Wong
145 (left) photo: Kailey Wong, model: Shoshana; (right) photo: Kaisik Wong, model: Merle Bulato